Violence against Women in Pornography

Violence against Women in Pornography illuminates the ways in which adult pornography hurts many women, both on and off screen. A growing body of social scientific knowledge shows that it is strongly associated with various types of violence against women in intimate relationships. Many women who try to leave abusive and/or patriarchal men also report that pornography plays a role in the abuse inflicted on them by their ex-partners. On top of these harms, male pornography consumption is strongly correlated with attitudes supporting violence against women. Many researchers, practitioners, and policy makers believe that adult pornography is a major problem and offer substantial evidence supporting this claim.

Violence against Women in Pornography, unlike books written mainly for scholarly and general audiences, specifically targets students enrolled in undergraduate criminology, deviance, women's and gender studies, masculinities studies, human sexuality, and media studies courses. Thoughtful discussion questions are placed at the end of each chapter, and appropriate PowerPoint slides and suggestions for classroom exercises will be available to aid student understanding. The main objective of this book is to motivate readers to think critically about adult pornography and to take progressive steps individually and collectively to curb the production and consumption of hurtful sexual media, including that from the "dark side of the Internet."

Walter S. DeKeseredy is Anna Deane Carlson Endowed Chair of Social Sciences, Professor of Sociology, and Director of the Research Center on Violence at West Virginia University. He has published 21 books and more than 130 scientific journal articles and book chapters on violence against women and other social problems. DeKeseredy is the recipient of many prestigious awards. In 2008, the Institute on Violence, Abuse, and Trauma gave him the Linda Saltzman Memorial Intimate Partner Violence Researcher Award. He received the University of Ontario Institute of Technology's inaugural Research Excellence Award in 2007. In addition, he jointly received the 2004 Distinguished Scholar Award from the American Society of Criminology's (ASC) Division on Women and Crime. ASC's Division on Critical Criminology gave him the Critical Criminologist of the Year Award in 1995 and the Lifetime Achievement Award in 2008. In 2014, the Academy of Criminal Justice Science's (ACJS) Critical Criminal Justice Section honored him with the Critical Criminal Justice Scholar Award.

Marilyn Corsianos is Professor of Criminology and Sociology at Eastern Michigan University. Corsianos's research interests include institutions of social control, public and private policing, and power and violence. She has studied the police in the United States and Canada focusing on police ethics and corruption, gender issues, detectives, discretionary powers, and community policing. She is committed to pursuing social change by identifying exclusionary practices in the production of knowledge, and identifying more equitable policing systems. She has published three books in addition to *Violence against Women in Pornography*, including one on policing and gendered justice, which won a CHOICE Outstanding Title Award. In 2015, in recognition of her research, she received the prestigious Ronald W. Collins Distinguished Faculty Award, which is the highest honor a faculty member can receive at Eastern Michigan University. In addition, she received the 2015 Distinguished Scholar Award, from the American Society of Criminology's (ASC) Division on Women and Crime.

Some readers will be enraged by this book, some will be shocked, and some will be inspired to activism—all for different reasons. DeKeseredy and Corsianos do what good authors should do: Provoke readers to think about and debate topics outside their "comfort zone." And the book is even more important because the target audience is college students, a population with high rates of pornography consumption and sexual violence.

Claire M. Renzetti, *University of Kentucky*

Few books on the topic of porn are as bold or far-reaching as this one. By tackling the issue of porn from multi-paradigmatic perspectives, *Violence against Women in Pornography* provides teachers and students alike with a rich and rigorous analysis of how porn undermines women's humanity, safety, and equality.

Gail Dines, *Wheelock College*

Violence against Women in Pornography

Walter S. DeKeseredy and
Marilyn Corsianos

Routledge
Taylor & Francis Group

NEW YORK AND LONDON

First published 2016
by Routledge
711 Third Avenue, New York, NY 10017

and by Routledge
2 Park Square, Milton Park, Abingdon, Oxon, OX14 4RN

Routledge is an imprint of the Taylor & Francis Group, an informa business

© 2016 Taylor & Francis

Library of Congress Cataloging in Publication Data
A catalog record for this book has been requested

ISBN: 978-1-138-95878-4 (hbk)
ISBN: 978-1-4557-7542-2 (pbk)
ISBN: 978-1-315-65255-9 (ebk)

Typeset in Times New Roman, Futura and Scala Sans
by Florence Production Ltd, Stoodleigh, Devon, UK

Contents

Foreword

LET'S get this out of the way right from the start—it's not anti-sex to be critical of pornography, especially the "gonzo" porn that is marketed primarily to boys and men, or to be concerned about its effects. It's just not. The porn industry and its defenders want you to believe that, of course, because they have a product to sell. They have a gigantic financial self-interest in keeping the gravy train flowing, so naturally they want to minimize criticism, and whenever possible delegitimize it.

The best way to do that with a product associated with sex is to claim that people who have a problem with it must either be 1) prudish, uptight, or sexually repressed, 2) a religious zealot, or 3) a self-righteous censor who does not appreciate the importance of free speech and the First Amendment.

I want to address these claims one at a time, in a spirit of honest exchange, and do so in a way that integrates scholarly analysis with personal experience. Because for me and almost everyone I know, pornography and its uses and abuses *is* personal. In some cases, profoundly personal. But before I get to that, I need to provide some context about the kind of work I do, and what that has to do with porn.

I have long been active in the multiracial, multiethnic and increasingly global movement to engage men in the fight to end men's violence against women. I've started anti-sexist men's organizations. I created the first large-scale program to enlist sports culture in the fight against sexual assault and relationship abuse. My colleagues and I have worked extensively with the US military—all services—for nearly two decades. Over the years I've done a lot of writing and public speaking on topics related to men, women, sex and violence.

My scholarly work has examined the ways in which social norms underlie abusive behaviors, including men's mistreatment of women. In other words, instead of seeing a problem like sexual assault as one in which a small number of sick or deviant individuals carry out a horrific crime, I'm interested in the various belief systems that condone and sometimes even encourage abusive acts. Most men who assault women are not one-dimensional ogres or sociopathic monsters. This is certainly true of male college students who commit sexual assault. In most cases they're disturbingly normal.

This prompts the question: if male children are not born biologically programmed or genetically predisposed to commit violent acts against women, then why do so many men end up doing just that? Why is men's violence against women such a big problem in our society and all over the world? And if most men who perpetrate these crimes are otherwise normal guys, what does it mean to be normal? What are the means by which societal norms are produced and reproduced? More specifically, what forces in male culture shape men's attitudes toward women, and how do those attitudes affect behavior?

Nearly two decades ago one of the co-authors of this book, Walter DeKeseredy, along with his colleague Martin Schwartz, examined one key aspect of this from a sociological perspective: the role of male peer support in condoning or encouraging sexist abuse. What role do friends, teammates, classmates, fraternity brothers and others play in this? To what extent are men conforming to, rather than transgressing, group norms when they aggress against women? In one particularly timely and useful discussion in this volume, DeKeseredy and Corsianos apply the male peer support framework to the topic of porn use by college men.

More broadly, they raise questions throughout the book about the underlying causes of men's violence against women: how much relative weight should be given to individual factors (e.g. neurochemical imbalances, personality disorders) and how much to social and environmental factors? How do sociological insights about the effects of porn differ from those generated by more individualistic psychological theories and studies?

We can't adequately explore those questions here, but I would like to propose that any serious examination of a phenomenon as widespread as men's violence against women has to include analysis of a range of societal factors. Consider an analogy. Can any serious person in the twenty-first century maintain that racism is an individual pathology, and not a much larger problem rooted in institutional structures and practices? Sure, let's hold individuals accountable for racist acts. But let's not pretend those acts spring from the unique characteristics of the perpetrator.

And so it is with sexism, which brings us to the topic at hand. When I first heard that the authors had written this book, my initial reaction was relief. Finally, someone had pulled together the most up-to-date theory and research about the relationship between pornography and violence against women, brought it together in one volume, and delivered it in a way that college students could digest and debate. It's about time.

For many of us who work in the gender violence prevention field, pornography has long been the 800-pound gorilla in the room. Few people even want to acknowledge it, much less criticize and deconstruct it. In countless sexual assault prevention workshops and presentations, we talk freely about the sexual objectification of women in media, and how this helps to desensitize men to women's core humanity. When you reduce someone to an object it becomes easier to dismiss them, mistreat them, and ultimately to violate their bodily integrity. We have no problem talking about all of this when it comes to advertising, Hollywood films or music videos. But when it comes to porn, we rarely even bring it up.

Meanwhile, a soulless, multibillion-dollar industry with disturbingly close financial ties to "respectable" multinational corporations continues to crank out thousands of videos annually that feature some of the most dehumanizing and degrading acts ever captured on film. Videos that are marketed directly to heterosexual men, in which scene after scene depicts men aggressively taunting and ridiculing women even as they penetrate them mercilessly, with little regard for the women's bodily health, and no regard for their sexual pleasure. And because of the internet, boys have access to this material at the tender age of ten or eleven; before they've even kissed a girl, millions of young boys have watched videos online of men ejaculating onto women's faces as they call them "cum-guzzling whores" who got what they deserved.

Many people in the sexual assault prevention world don't want to talk about any of this for a variety of reasons. They don't feel confident they have the knowledge or vocabulary to discuss the subject intelligently. They know that some men (and women) can get defensive and hostile if they're criticized for using porn. They know that discussions about how and why some women choose to do porn often evoke strong feelings and generate conflict. And of course some educators steer clear of this subject matter because they are loathe to be thought of as unhip or uptight. And so the sounds of silence prevail.

But not here. The authors of this book are committed to presenting a range of findings and theoretical frameworks about porn and its relation to sexual assault, sexual abuse and domestic violence. They also don't shy away from including discussions about the racism openly displayed in contemporary porn. The reader is invited to sift through all of this and come to your own conclusions. This fearless approach has the added benefit of respecting the intelligence and moral agency of students. No need to shelter you from the data. If you're mature enough to consume porn (whether or not you do), you ought to be able to handle some critical thinking about it.

Which brings me, finally, to the earlier discussion about how the porn industry and its defenders try to dismiss criticism. Let's address briefly the claims they make about their critics.

They're prudish, uptight, or sexually repressed.

No, we're not. I can speak for myself most authoritatively on this point, but I know I speak for many people—women and men—when I say that my objections to the mainstream of (heterosexual) porn are not about the sex, but the sexism. Is it possible to produce sexually explicit material that does not reinforce misogynous beliefs about women's (or men's) sexuality? Sure, but that's not even close to what the vast majority of guys are consuming today, or for the foreseeable future. In a world where each year men harass, abuse, rape and murder literally millions of women and girls, it is not prudish to object to an industry that sexualizes men's power over women, and then has the chutzpah to pretend that the women really enjoy it. It's not prudish to object to that; it's an important political act, not to mention common human decency.

They're religious zealots.

No, we're not. Are there some people whose objection to porn is rooted in their religious beliefs? Of course, and I respect that, even if I might not agree with the theology or even the moral teaching at its foundation. But I know a lot of people who are terribly concerned about the deep misogyny in mainstream porn culture, and few of them are motivated by religious beliefs. Instead, they are driven by a passion for social and gender justice, and a longing for a world where all women and men—and everyone else—are treated with respect and dignity.

They're censors who don't respect the First Amendment.

No, we're not. I believe in free speech as much as anyone else. And let's be clear: the porn industry hardly suffers from an inability to exercise its free speech rights. In fact, in the debate about porn that has taken place in our society over the past forty years, the purveyors of porn have had a much louder voice than their critics—especially their feminist critics—because they have the money to purchase the platform and the big megaphone. When it comes to porn, we don't need less free speech; we need more. For example, one can only hope that in coming years, more young Americans—especially men—who claim to be committed to gender equality and racial justice find the courage to speak out about the blatant misogyny and racism in gonzo porn.

So think about this book as an invaluable contribution to free speech. It gives voice to a multitude of concerns many people have had for a long time about the relationship between porn culture and the ongoing problem of men's violence against women. It doesn't have all the answers; no one does. But it asks the reader—you—to look at this issue through a critical lens. At a minimum, you will come away with a wealth of valuable insight about the personal and societal implications of porn.

Jackson Katz, Ph.D.

Preface

At the time of writing this preface, much political, media, and scholarly attention was bestowed upon campus sexual assaults in both the United States and Canada. As a matter of fact, this problem was considered to be of such importance that President Barack Obama officially established the White House Task Force to Protect Students From Sexual Assault on January 22, 2014. Furthermore, north of the U.S. border, in mid March of 2015, Ontario Premier Kathleen Wynne announced that community colleges and universities will be required by law to create sexual assault policies that must be updated and renewed every four years. As well, student input into these policies is mandatory and Ontario institutions of higher learning must now publicly reveal rates of sexual violence and have transparent complaint procedures and response protocols.

Like others who, for decades, have worked in the area of gendered violence and violations, our response was, "Good, but it is about time!" Why did it take so long for political leaders to listen to what feminist scholars, practitioners, and activists have been telling them for years? Sexual assaults committed by male undergraduate students constitute one of the most significant threats to female students' health and well-being. Actually, we have known, since the late 1980s, that at least one out of every four female undergraduates will experience some type of sexual victimization during their university/college career. It is beyond the scope of this book to answer the above question, but it cannot be emphasized enough that the North American policy makers' silence over the years was deafening. The same can be said about the selective inattention that many of them gave to other forms of woman abuse, such as sexual harassment, violent "hook ups," male physical and psychological assaults on female marital/cohabiting partners, and stalking. There are, of course, other harms women experience, but they are made explicit in subsequent parts of this book and numerous other publications.

Regardless of politicians' reluctance to address violence against women, the feminist research, activist, and practitioner communities are still actively involved in collectively sensitizing the world to the breadth, distribution, key sources, and outcomes of various types of violence against women. However, compared to other determinants of this harm, such as age, sexist attitudes and beliefs, patriarchal male peer support, race/ethnicity and intimate relationship status, male consumption of violent and racist pornography has received short shrift. This is hardly a trivial problem, given that a growing body of international research reviewed in this book reveals that such media are strongly *correlated* with the abuse of women in intimate heterosexual relationships. We do not assert that such pornography is a direct cause of sexual assault, beatings, stalking, and other forms of gendered violence, but it is definitely a major risk factor, one that is only destined to become more powerful in years to come.

Violence Against Women in Pornography has several main objectives, one of which is to review the extant conceptual, theoretical, empirical, and policy literature on the topic. Another goal is to motivate more people, especially men, to think critically about porn and to take progressive steps individually and collectively to curb the production and consumption of hurtful sexual media. Additionally, we hope that our book will serve as an instructional aid for those who teach courses on pornography, media, gender studies, violence against women, criminology, and the sociology of deviance.

Chapter 1 describes the extent and distribution of pornography use and production. A key point made there is that the consumption of porn is not an occasional pastime for a handful of "sick" people. Rather, it is an integral part of an alarming number of people's daily lives in this current era. Certainly, the Internet makes viewing porn easier and cheaper than ever before and we anticipate that consumption rates will escalate rapidly as porn becomes even more acceptable among mainstream society. It is, indeed, rare not to find someone who has been exposed to sexual media in some capacity.

Chapter 2 focuses on the nature of today's pornography. Special attention is devoted to describing the contemporary pornography industry, which continues to grow in size and strength. In fact, there will be thousands more Internet porn sites by the time you finish reading this book. We must warn you that some parts of this chapter, are rather disturbing as are other sections of the book. Yet, we cannot emphasize enough that our work does not attempt to border on "shock theater."

Chapter 3 provides sociological answers to two questions: why do men use porn and what are the effects of their consumption. A few recent individualistic explanations are also summarized and critiqued.

We are among a relatively small international cadre of academics who examine how violent and degrading pornography contributes to women's experiences of violence in private places. Our work and that of our colleagues is reviewed in Chapter 4. Violence against women in the pornography industry and pornography cyber-bullying are also examined. New directions in research, too, are suggested.

Chapter 5 outlines some progressive policy proposals. As Robert Jensen reminds us in his 2007 seminal scholarly monograph *Getting Off: Pornography and the End of Masculinity*, "We have a lot of work to do."

We fully expect that this book will make many people uncomfortable, given that pornography use is so widespread and has become normalized. Discomfort, though, is a good thing and has led many people to take a journey that they never anticipated taking. It is often said that "a leopard can't change its spots," but the good news is that more and more people now recognize the dangers associated with violent porn use and distribution. Even so, more participants in the struggle to eliminate the objectification and degradation of women in the media are needed. Please join us if you haven't already.

Acknowledgments

FIRST and foremost, we would like to thank our Acquisitions Editor Pam Chester for working closely with us on this project. We greatly appreciate her courage and commitment. Many other people in her shoes would not want to take on a "hot potato" like this book, but Pam had faith and we will always remember her kindness and professionalism.

Our Development Editor Ellen Boyne also played a key role in the completion of this book. Ellen is a true friend of the authors and the publishing world is a better place because of her.

Irene Bunnell, also affiliated with Routledge, did an excellent job of copy editing. We thank her for her patience and guidance.

A very special thank you goes out to John Foubert, Rus Funk and James Ptacek who took time away from their very busy schedules to read drafts of two chapters. They helped make this book better than it otherwise would have been.

Books are typically products of a collective effort. This one is no exception. Over the years, we have greatly benefitted from the comments, criticisms, lessons, support, and influences of these progressive friends and colleagues: Kristine Ajrouch, Rowland Atkinson, Bernie Auchter, Karen Bachar, Ronet Bachman, Gregg Barak, Ola Barnett, Joanne Belknap, Raquel Bergen, Helene Berman, David Bird, Rebecca Block, Ana Bridges, Avi Brisman, Gerhard Boomgaarden, Ana Bridges, Carrie Buist, Liqun Cao, Steve Cake, Gail Caputo, Gary Cassagnol, Susan Caringella, Pat Carlen, Kerry Carrington, Meda Chesney-Lind, Ann Coker, Elizabeth Comack, Kimberly Cook, Terry Cox, Wesley Crichlow, Francis T. Cullen, Elliott Currie, Kathleen Daly, Juergen Dankwort, Jodie Death, Gail Dines, Joseph F. Donnermeyer, Molly Dragiewicz, Desmond Ellis, Richard V. Ericson, Karlene Faith, Jeff Ferrell, Bonnie Fisher, William F. Flack Jr., Diane Follingstad, David O. Friedrichs, Rus Funk, Alberto Godenzi, Edward Gondolf, Judith Grant, Steve Hall, Amanda Hall-Sanchez, Barbara Hart, Keith Hayward, Ronald Hinch, Sandra Huntzinger, Nancy Jurik, Rita Kanarek, Peter Kraska, David Kauzlarich, Dorie Klein, Clifford Jansen, Victor Kappeler, Mary Koss, Salley Laskey, Paul Leighton, Julian Lo, Michael J. Lynch, Brian MacLean, Eugene McLaughlin, Anne Menard, James Messerschmidt, Raymond Michalowski, Jody Miller, Susan L. Miller, Dragan Milovanovic, Ruth Morris, Louise Moyer, Christopher Mullins, Kyle Mulrooney, Roslyn Muraskin,

Darlene Murphy, Stephen Muzzatti, Robynne Neugebauer, Nancy Neylon, James Nolan, Patrik Olsson, Sue Osthoff, Reiko Ozaki, Sandy Ortman, Barbara Owen, Ellen Pence, Ruth Peterson, Lori Post, Gary Potter, Tim Prenzler, Mike Presdee, Jeffrey Reiman, Callie Rennison, Barbara Richardson, Robin Robinson, Jeffrey Ian Ross, Dawn Rothe, Linda Saltzman, Daniel Saunders, Martin Schwartz, Donna Selman, Aysan Sev'er, Solange Simoes, Susan Sharp, Michael D. Smith, Natalie Sokoloff, Betsy Stanko, Cris Sullivan, Thomas Sutton, Kenneth Tunnell, Neil Websdale, Louise Westmarland, David Wiesenthal, Simon Winlow, Jock Young, and Joan Zorza. Since many of these people disagree with one another, we accept full responsibility for the information presented in this book.

As always, our strongest thanks go to our loved ones. Walter is especially grateful for the ongoing support of Pat and Andrea DeKeseredy, as well as that of his "fur children." And, Marilyn would especially like to thank Spiro Vlahos and Rena and Demetre Vlahos-Corsianos for their unconditional love and support.

Chapter 1

The Extent and Distribution of Pornography Use and Production

In the space of a generation, a product that once was available in the back alleys of big cities has gone corporate, delivered now directly into homes and hotel rooms by some of the biggest companies in the United States. It is estimated that Americans now spend somewhere around $10 billion a year on adult entertainment, which is as much as they spend attending professional sporting events, buying music or going out to the movies.

(Leung, 2012, p. 22)

PORNOGRAPHY is widely used, produced, and distributed around the world. Consumption of porn is not a rare act committed by a small group of pathological people. Pornography consumption in the United States has steadily increased over the years (Maltz and Maltz, 2008; Paul, 2005; Sarracino and Scott, 2008). According to *Internet Pornography Statistics*, there are 4.2 million pornographic websites (12 percent of total websites), and 68 million daily pornographic search engine requests which account for 25 percent of total requests. Also, 42.7 percent of all Internet users view pornography; 34 percent of average users receive unwanted pornographic exposure; and the average age of first Internet exposure to porn is 11 years. Moreover, every second $3075.64 is spent on pornography, and every 39 minutes a new pornographic video is created in the United States.

Internet pornography comprises approximately 12 percent of the Internet and is a multi-billion dollar business (Edelman, 2009). According to the Internet Filter Learning Center (2008), 13 percent of the U.S. population regularly views porn online, and nearly 75 percent of the viewers are male; and in 2006, pornography consumers in the United States spent $13.3 billion out of a worldwide take of $100 billion dollars. The Internet Filter Software Review also reports that "sex," "porn," and "XXX" are among the top most commonly searched terms on the World Wide Web.

Porn sites get more traffic than major search engines including Google, Yahoo, and MSN (Web Pro News, 2004). Commercially produced Internet porn is easily accessible and cheaply available or free. Videos and later DVDs sparked the growth of the pornography market throughout the 1980s and 1990s, but since the 1990s, the Internet has undoubtedly expanded the porn industry in unprecedented ways. Porn viewers today have many options in accessing porn that include buying or renting DVDs, buying video-on-demand on cable, and streaming videos over the Internet. Porn can be bought and consumed in private and can be viewed anywhere and at any time. For example, the cell phone market for porn reached $775 million in Europe in 2007, and $27 million in the United States (Carew, 2008).

According to Kimmel (2008), the gross sales of porn media in the United States today range from $10 and $14 billion annually, making the porn industry bigger than the revenues of ABC, NBC, and CBS combined. And, from the 1000 most visited online sites, 100 are adult-sex oriented. He further adds that

> sales and rentals of pornographic videos and DVDs alone gross about $4 billion a year. More than 260 new pornographic videos are produced every week. Adult bookstores outnumber McDonald's restaurants in the United States by a margin of at least three to one. On the Internet, pornography has increased 1,800 percent, from 14 million web pages in 1998 to 260 million in 2003 and 1.5 billion downloads per month in 2005.
>
> (p. 170)

Jensen (2007) notes that there are no absolutely reliable statistics on the industry's revenues, but annual sales in the United States are often estimated at $10 billion or higher and worldwide revenues are estimated to be around $57 billion. "For comparative purposes, the Hollywood box office—the amount of money Americans spent to go out to the movies—was $9 billion in 2005" (Jensen, 2007, p. 80). Pornography today has moved from a profitable underground business, which often was interconnected with organized crime, to a profitable industry that has become increasingly more mainstream and includes both small producers as well as large multi-billion dollar corporations.

It seems that the industry today cannot keep up with the demand by consumers for more porn overall, as well as more extreme porn that depicts outright brutality and denigration of women. Jensen (2007) notes:

> In 2005, 13,588 new hard-core video/DVD titles were released, a number that has risen steadily since statistics were first kept. Another difference is in the level of misogyny. While many types of images throughout human history have objectified, marginalized, or denigrated women, there is nothing comparable to the deluge of woman-hating products of the contemporary pornography industry.
>
> (p. 81)

Viewers can't seem to get enough, and more extreme and violent forms of porn are being demanded. Interestingly, Al Cooper, a Stanford University psychologist who studies cyber-sex addiction reports that 20 percent of porn surfers today are addicts, and treatment centers across the country are reporting an increase in number of patients who are addicted or negatively impacted by Internet pornography.

Technology has certainly made porn more accessible. The introduction of the VCR in the 1980s meant that pornography could be made available on video tapes and played at home. The number of porn videos made in the 1980s and 1990s increased drastically, and the Internet use that followed also meant that consumers of porn could view the material in the privacy of their homes, but now they had access to more in terms of overall quantity, as well as in the types of genres. According to a 2006 article in *XBIZ*, an online industry trade magazine:

> For years, the adult market has led online sales by providing the market with hundreds of thousands of choices and has rightfully led the way in selling content online. Subscription models, affiliate programs, and many other new business modes were either invented or perfected by the adult webmaster. . . . As recently as five years ago, the adult market produced 75 percent of all cash that was spent with online services.
>
> (Crockett, 2006)

There is no denying that porn images are widespread and available through a number of mediums: on laptops and PCs, cell phones, iPods and iPads, as well as other digital-video communication technologies. There is also no denying the accessibility of porn as a result of the Internet.

Beginning with home computers and Internet access in the 1990s to today's commonly used "smart phones," IPads, tablets, etc. . . . pornography can be accessed 24/7 from both national and international sites and be done with a certain level of anonymity. There are millions of sites to choose from including both free and paid sites. The accessibility, affordability, and relative anonymity have fueled the consumption of online pornography (Cooper, 2004). According to Waskul (2004):

> At its core, what is most new about Internet sex is its unprecedented access. Never before have so many people had such easy access to so much sexually explicit material. Previous technologies made sexually explicit materials available, but adult movie theaters, pornographic bookstores, the dank and dimly lit back room of neighborhood video rental shops, the embarrassment of purchasing a nudie magazine at a local gas station, and similar controls have always kept the availability of these materials somewhat limited and rather tightly confined. The Internet has significantly changed that. From the comfort of one's home and under a dense veil of anonymity, an enormous range of sex is ready available at one's fingertips.
>
> (p. 4)

By the end of September 2009, a quarter of the world's population had access to the Internet, a 380 percent increase from 2000 (www.interent worldstats.com/stats. htm). The percentage of U.S. Internet users rose from 44 percent to 74 percent from

2000 to 2009 (www.internetworldstats.com/am/us.htm). China's Internet users are estimated at 457 million with more than 303 million (66.2 percent of all users) connecting via cell phones (Chinese Internet Network Information Center survey data, 2010) making porn readily available 24/7. The Chinese government has attempted to police online pornography through a number of anti-pornography campaigns, but despite its efforts, the number of registered porn website members and visits to porn websites appear to have increased over the years (Liang and Lu, 2012). Liang and Lu (2012) assert that the number of Chinese who visit porn sites each year is in the millions. They further add that

> domestic porn site organizers and managers increasingly utilized computer servers abroad to avoid police detection, and by the end of 2009, official statistics showed that close to 80 percent of porn site servers were stationed abroad, with the United States as the leading exporter.
>
> (p. 118)

Moreover,

> in August 2009 . . . the police in Jiangsu province cracked a major case in which one of the top three Chinese porn servers stationed in the United States was utilized to serve thirteen porn sites in China with 12 million registered members.
>
> (p. 118)

Journalists in many Western Industrialized countries have frequently covered the topic of porn availability on the Internet and have often implied that porn consumption might be an age-specific issue with the biggest audience being adolescents, a group largely seen as being impressionable given their lack of social experiences, and therefore particularly susceptible to the influences of pornographic images. Research conducted to date appears to find that pornography consumption has become an everyday phenomenon for adolescents in industrialized nations. Studies done in the United States, Netherlands, U.K., Germany, France, and Singapore indicate that between two-fifths and two-thirds of adolescents have already viewed porn online (Conseil Superieur de l'Audiovisuel, 2004; Icon Kids and Youth, 2009; Liau et al., 2008; Livingstone and Helsper, 2010; Peter and Valkenburg, 2006; Wolak et al., 2007). In Weber, Quiring and Daschmann's (2012) study, 352 German adolescents between the ages of 16 and 19 were recruited for an online survey on pornography consumption and its developmental correlates. The study found pronounced gender differences in participants' use of pornography. Sixty-one percent of females and 93 percent of male participants indicated that they had already viewed pornographic video clips or films. Another 20 percent of girls and 5 percent of boys had done so "only by accident," and the remaining 19 percent of girls and 2 percent of boys had not done so at all. However, only 3 percent of all female participants had viewed porn video clips or films "(almost) daily" or "several times a day" in the previous 6 months, and 27 percent viewed porn weekly or on a monthly basis. On the other hand, 47 percent of boys watched porn video clips "(almost) daily" or "several times a day," and 38 percent reported weekly or monthly use. Another observed gender difference was in adolescents' perceptions of whether their friends watched porn. For instance, 86 percent of boys, whereas only 35 percent of girls assumed that most of their friends had viewed pornography.

Significant gender differences in prevalence rates of porn consumption, as well as consumption patterns, were found in Hald's (2006) study of young, heterosexual Danish adults. A national survey was conducted using a representative sample of 688 heterosexual adult men and women between the ages of 18 and 30. Pornography in this study was defined as follows (2006, p. 579): "Any kind of material aiming at creating or enhancing sexual feelings or thoughts in the recipient and, at the same time (1) containing explicit exposure and/or descriptions of the genitals and (2) clear and explicit sexual acts such as vaginal intercourse, anal intercourse, oral sex, masturbation, bondage, sadomasochism (SM), rape, urine sex, animal sex, etc. It was emphasized that materials containing men and women posing or acting naked such as seen in Playboy/Playgirl did not contain clear and explicit sexual acts and were to be disregarded as pornography when completing the questionnaire." Not surprisingly, men were exposed to porn at a younger age in comparison to women and consumed more porn as measured by time and frequency, and used porn more frequently during sexual activity on their own. For example, 97.8 percent of men indicated they had "ever watched porn" in relation to 79.5 percent of women. From those who answered "yes" to ever watching porn, 92.2 percent of men and 60 percent of women indicated they watched porn within the last 6 months; 82.5 percent of men but 33.6 percent of women viewed porn in the last month; 63.4 percent of men but, 13.6 percent of women in the last week; and 26.2 percent of men but only 3.1 percent of women in the last 24 hours. Also, differences in the frequency of use included the following: 28.8 percent of men but only 11.4 percent of women indicated they viewed porn 1–2 times per week, and 38.8 percent of men but only 6.9 percent of women viewed porn three times per week or more.

Additionally there was a significant gender difference in the average time of use per week (actual time spent viewing porn). Women viewed porn more often with a regular sexual partner whereas men viewed porn often on their own or with friends who were non-sexual partners. Also, men preferred a wider variety of hardcore versus softcore porn in relation to women. Men were much more likely to view porn that depicted anal intercourse, oral sex, group sex involving one man and two or more women, lesbian sex, and amateur sex. Women, on the other hand were much more likely to prefer softcore porn and group sex that involved one woman with more men. The author notes that despite Denmark's more liberal attitudes towards sex and pornography, in recent years there has been growing public, political, and scientific concern about the prevalence and effects of porn consumption and more research is being demanded in this area.

High porn consumption among men overall in relation to women was also found in a Swedish study (Lewis et al., 1996), but age was also relevant. Men, especially younger males consumed porn to a greater extent than women; but young women (18–24) consumed more than older men (50–65 years of age). Another Swedish study (Rogala and Tyden, 1999) surveyed 1000 young women and found that four out of five had consumed porn; and one-third believed that porn had influenced their sexual behavior. But, a more recent study (Haggstrom-Nordin et al., 2005) of 718 students from 47 high school classes in a medium-sized Swedish city, found that 86 percent ($n = 603$) of the students had ever consumed pornography; more males (98 percent, $n = 370$) than women (72 percent, $n = 233$). The study further found that that the Internet and cable TV were the most common sources. When students were asked how they categorized the kind of pornographic material they consumed, most (58 percent, $n = 419$) said "soft porn," 31 percent ($n = 220$) said "hard porn" and 3 percent ($n = 19$) described it as "violent porn." Also:

> more men (75 percent, $n = 291$) than women (19 percent, $n = 62$) took the initiative to consume pornography and 83 percent ($n = 390$) watched pornography at home. In all, 71 percent ($n = 500$) believed that pornography influenced others' sexual behavior, whereas 29 percent ($n = 203$) stated that they had been influenced themselves.

(p. 103)

Furthermore, a Swedish study on the porn consumption of male adolescents found that 96 percent of the 16-year-old boys surveyed had watched porn, and that 10 percent viewed porn everyday (identified as "frequent users"). The mean age of actively searching for porn was 12.3 years. Also, frequent users were three times more likely to think about sex all the time, and a higher proportion had fantasized and often tried sexual acts seen in porn (Mattebo et al., 2013).

Similarly, gender differences in porn consumption were also found in the United States (Carroll et al., 2008). College men were more likely to have ever viewed pornography compared to women (87 vs. 31 percent). Almost 50 percent of the male respondents reported using porn every week in comparison to only 3.2 percent of the women. Also, Boies (2002) found that in samples of young people, men viewed pornography three times more often than women, and in samples of older men and women, the rate increased to 6:1. Looking at Internet pornography specifically, Boies found somewhat similar numbers to Carroll et al. (2008); 72 percent of college men and 24 percent of college women reported consuming pornography with 11 percent of users consuming porn once a week or more.

On the other hand, Wright's study (2013) examined U.S. males' consumption of pornography using cross-sectional General Social Survey (GSS) data gathered between 1973 and 2010. The GSS is the only ongoing, national, full-probability, interview-survey that examines people's social beliefs and behaviors in the United States (National Data Program, 2011). General Social Surveys are funded by the National Science Foundation and have been conducted in 1973–1978, 1980, 1982, 1983–1993, 1994, 1996, 1998, 2000, 2002, 2004, 2006, 2008, and 2010. The total number of male participants who responded to the question about pornography consumption in the years between 1973 and 2010 was 14,193. Four demographic predictors of pornography consumption were explored in Wright's study (2013), which included age, religiosity, ethnicity, and education. These variables were measured in all years participants' pornography consumption. Participants ranged from 18 to 89 years of age with the mean age being 44.7. Religiosity was operationalized as frequency of attendance at church services, and measured on a scale from 0 (never attended) to 8 (attended more than once per week). The mean was 3.41. Ethnicity was operationalized as White or non-White. Whites represented 83.3 percent of overall participants. Finally, education was operationalized in terms of the number of years of school participants had completed. The mean was 12.88.

Pornography consumption was measured by asking participants whether they had viewed a pornographic film in the prior year. Wright (2013) found that more U.S. males appear to be consuming porn today. For instance, 26 percent of the 1970s GSS participants reported they had consumed porn, in comparison to 34 percent of the participants between 2000 and 2010. Across all years, 30.8 percent of respondents reported they had viewed a porn film in the prior year.

However, at the same time, regression analyses showed that each new year brought about less than a .5 percent increase in the overall number of adult males who consumed porn. Therefore, the author concluded that the percentage of adult U.S. males who consume pornography appears to have increased only slightly over time despite the introduction of the Internet and porn accessibility. But, possible explanations for this could be that more males are consuming porn but their willingness to admit to it is only slightly increasing. The other and more plausible explanation is that males' consumption of porn films specifically has increased only slightly but their consumption of porn in the wide range of available mediums beyond "film" has increased.

Wright, Bae, and Funk (2013), on the other hand, looked specifically at U.S. women's exposure to pornography over four decades again utilizing the GSS data gathered between 1973 and 2010. As discussed above, the measure of porn exposure employed by the GSS consisted of asking whether one has or hasn't had any exposure to pornographic films in the prior year. The authors recognize some of the limitations in overall measurement of porn exposure with this approach, but also claim that this method allows for direct assessment of whether more U.S. women are consuming porn over time. They (2013) further add that "The GSS is national in scope, samples female adults of all ages, employs random sampling, and at each data collection focuses on the same medium, asks about the same time-span of exposure, and employs the same dichotomous index of exposure" (p. 1132).

Some critics, however, argue that the number may be low given the more common viewing of porn on the Internet and therefore question the validity in assessing pornographic movie viewing. The authors, on the other hand, insist that several sources suggest that it is indeed valid. They assert that pornographic movies can be streamed online from a variety of websites (e.g., adultrental.com, adultvicdonetwork.com, moviemonster.com), and that some economic data indicate that pornographic video sales and rentals continue to be the preferred method of consumption in the United States (Bridges et al., 2010). And, that in 2000, 2002, and 2004, in addition to asking about pornographic movie viewing, the GSS also asked participants whether they had viewed Internet pornography. In sum, the GSS data showed that 16 percent of women indicated they had viewed a pornographic movie while 4 percent indicated they had viewed Internet pornography. The data did not suggest that there had been a linear increase in the percentage of U.S. women who consume pornography. But, when looking at the percentage of women aged 18–30 who consumed pornography, GSS data suggests a slight overall increase over time and that increased access to the Internet in the mid-1990s resulted in a more stable percentage of younger female pornography consumers (Wright, Bae, and Funk, 2013).

But, as mentioned above, others speculate that these numbers are low given the limitations with the measurement of porn consumption. For instance, Vivid, one of the world's largest adult film companies, in 2007 experienced a 35 percent drop in DVD sales but more demand for other forms of technology such as Vivid's websites and pay-per-view services on television and online (Brewer, 2008).

Interestingly, higher numbers of porn consumption among women were reported by Fox (2006) who focused specifically on viewing online porn. It found that 28.7 percent of undergraduate college women had visited sexually explicit websites with video content either ever or once or twice a year.

In addition to studies on the amount of porn consumption, levels of acceptance of porn have been examined. Carroll, Padilla-Walker, Nelson, Olson, Barry, and Madsen (2008), for instance, examined pornography use and acceptance of emerging adults ages 18–26. They surveyed 813 university students (500 of which were women) from six college sites across the United States, and found that 67 percent of young men and 49 percent of young women agree that viewing porn is acceptable. But, almost 9 out of 10 young men reported using porn in comparison to less than one-third (31 percent) of young women. Also, nearly half of the men reported that they viewed porn at least weekly and about 1 in 5 reported that they viewed porn daily or every other day. Only about 1 in 10 women, on the other hand, viewed porn with any regularity.

Alternatively, other studies indicate that porn consumers also recognize that viewing can be problematic. In an anonymous online survey of 84 college-age males in the United States, Twohig, Crosby, and Cox (2009) found that approximately 20–60 percent of the sample who viewed porn found it to be problematic depending on the domain of interest. Approximately 50 percent of the males in the sample viewed online pornography, and depending on the domain of interest, approximately 20–60 percent of those who reported viewing indicated that viewing was problematic. Viewing porn had the strongest negative effects in the psychological/spiritual domain and on actual behavioral outcomes such as problems at work or school or damaged relationships. Negative outcomes did not increase with increased viewing. Rather, significant differences were only seen between participants who viewed porn and those that did not, but the authors recognize that this is most likely the result of limitations of the question used to measure viewing; that is, it only asked participants the number of times they had viewed, but not the amount of time spent viewing.

INCREASED DISTRIBUTION AND CONSUMPTION OF HURTFUL SEXUAL MEDIA = MAINSTREAMING OF VIOLENCE AGAINST WOMEN

In recent years, the genre of porn called "gonzo" has dominated the mainstream commercial porn market. There are two major styles of mass marketed heterosexual porn films: "features" and "gonzo." "Pornographic features mimic, however badly, the conventions of a Hollywood movie. There is some minimal plot, character development, and dialogue, all in the service of presenting the explicit sex. Gonzo films have no such pretention; they are simply recorded sex, often in a private home or on some minimal set" (Jensen, 2007, p. 55). Gonzo has become increasingly popular over the years. Acts shown in feature films are also featured in gonzo but are often performed with more aggression, often with more than one man involved but one woman, and with more denigrating language against the woman. Gonzo contains sex scene after sex scene with no plot or story line. An article in Adult Video News (2005) reported that gonzo is "the overwhelmingly dominant porn genre since it's less expensive to produce than plot-oriented features." There has been increasing demand for gonzo because it provides the rougher material that consumers demand. Jensen (2007) quotes porn director Jules Jordan who discusses consumers' desires for a harsh gonzo market. He states:

> One of the things about today's porn and the extreme market, the gonzo market, so many fans want to see so much more extreme stuff that I'm always trying to figure out ways to do something different. But it seems everybody wants to see a girl doing a d.p. now or a gangbang. . . . a lot of fans are becoming a lot more demanding about wanting to see the more extreme stuff. It's definitely brought porn somewhere, but I don't know where it's headed from there.
>
> (p. 70)

Also, prior to the late 1980s and 1990s, anal sex was not often depicted in mainstream heterosexual porn. But by the late 1990s, it had become mainstream. Other sex acts that became popular in gonzo in the early 2000s, and slowly began to be introduced in features included double penetration (where a woman is penetrated vaginally and anally at the same time); double anal (where a woman is penetrated anally by two men at the same time; double vaginal (where a woman is penetrated vaginally by two men at the same time; and ass-to-mouth (ATM) (where a man removes his penis from a woman's anus and without cleaning it puts it in her mouth or the mouth of another woman) (Jensen, 2007). These images have become mainstream in the porn films and videos of today.

According to Dines (2010), in the world of porn, women "are astonishingly immune to being called cunts, whores, cumdumpsters, sluts, bitches, hot slits, fuck-tubes, squirty skanks, and stupid hoes." Moreover, she states that the porn world "is an uncomplicated world where women don't need equal pay, health care, day care, retirement plans, good schools for their children, or safe housing. It is a world filled with one-dimensional women who are nothing more than collections of holes" (p. xxiv).

Also, even though the "cum shot" has been promoted as the norm in mainstream pornography, the "rules" have changed in today's gonzo. In gonzo, men ejaculate into a woman's mouth followed by her allowing the semen to drip from her mouth, and then swallowing it. And, scenes with multiple female performers commonly have them passing the semen between them with their mouth. Additionally, "bukkake" (discussed in Chapter 2) has certainly become a common practice in gonzo where groups of men ejaculate into a woman's mouth or onto her face.

The mainstreaming of porn has meant that consumers today are less likely to "see it as dirty" or "deviant" and, as already discussed, the privacy of viewing in their own homes has meant that more people are likely to search and view porn online. Also, Dines (2010) reminds us that the visibility of porn in pop culture has helped strip away the stigma attached to the porn of earlier decades, and has allowed viewers to openly "flirt" with ideas they would not have considered otherwise. The popularity of porn stars such as Jenna Jameson where shows about her have appeared on E! Entertainment and VH1, as well as celebrities such as Howard Stern who frequently puts porn stars on his show are great examples provided by Dines (2010) of how pornography has infiltrated the mainstream culture by becoming inter-connected with mainstream companies and these have contributed to the growing consumption of porn. For example, in the cable television business,

> porn is distributed by Time Warner Cable, Fox Communication, and Comcast—the latter being the largest cable TV providers in the United States (Comcast also own E! Entertainment, a cable station that often carried porn-friendly documentaries, such as one on Jenna Jameson, as well as the show The Girls Next Door). . . . Pornography is also distributed via satellite TV, with one of the biggest companies, DirecTV, offering Playboys Spice Network and LFP Broadcasting's Hustler TV. . . . In 2006, the Liberty Media Group took control of DirecTV, and it also has part ownership in Sirius Radio, which carries the Howard Stern Show, a show that serves as an advertisement for the porn industry by regularly inviting porn stars.
>
> (Dines, 2010, pp. 51–52)

As well as porn producers such as Max Hardcore who was sentenced to almost 4 years in prison for violating federal obscenity laws (see Chapter 2).

As Journalist Pamela Paul in her book *Pornified* asserts, porn today "is so seamlessly integrated into popular culture that embarrassment or surreptitious-ness is no longer part of the equation." And, according to the *New York Times*, even the lines concerning pole-dancing have been blurred between its traditional place in strip clubs to its growing popularity in dance classes among suburban wives. Pole dancing was introduced as an erotic performance in Euro-American strip clubs in the 1980s, but began to move into the mainstream through the offering of pole-dancing exercise classes in the first decade of the millennium in both the United States and Britain (Holland and Attwood, 2009).

Today, the Internet has made it possible for people to access the most graphic sexual images with the click of a button and in an increasingly competitive market that remains patriarchal and misogynistic. Porn producers are continuously trying to "out-do" their competitors and throw any boundaries that may have existed right out of the playing field into unchartered territory. This has moved viewers of today's porn to greater acceptance of sexualized brutality and body-punishing sex. According to porn director and actor Bill Margold, his objective in the porn he and others produce is described as follows:

I'd like to really show what I believe the men want to see: violence against women. I firmly believe that we serve a purpose by showing that. The most violent we can get is the cum shot in the face. Men get off behind that, because they can get even with the women they can't have. We try to inundate the world with orgasms in the face.

(Strouer and Levine, 2007, p. 69)

One of the costs to this is described by Jackson Katz as follows (2006):

Because there is so little sexual content in media that is not pornographic, and because there is so little quality sex education in schools, pornography fills a void for millions of sexually inexperienced kids. What they see in pornography helps to establish a template for "normal" sexual behavior that they feel pressure to emulate. They might not initially be drawn to pornography because of all the misogyny and brutality, but that is what they are getting from the stories being depicted in most mainstream porn today.

(pp. 193–194)

The most common images that overwhelmingly cater to a straight male audience are images of women always ready for sex, always willing to please, and always sexually satisfied. The anti-pornography activist, John Stoltenberg,[1] writes that pornography "tells lies about women, though it tells the truth about men." Women are often portrayed in one-dimensional hyper-sexualized images without any "sexual agency"[2] (Corsianos, 2007); that is, always orgasmic, willing to do anything, often reacting by doing what they're told, or by being physically moved into position to perform in particular ways, always accepting of what is being done to them regardless of the level of humiliation or level of violence, and always wanting more. The fact that these images have become so mainstream with the audience wanting more tells us a lot about the fantasies of many straight males and/or the acceptance of these images.

But, according to Kimmel (2008), porn also tells lies about men:

—that sex is inevitably vile and degrading, an animal urge that propels men to fuse disgust and desire. Some lies may be ones men really want to hear, the majority one being that every woman really, severely, deep down, wants to have sex with you. In a sexual marketplace where they feel completely dominated by women—from women having the power to decide if you are going to get sex in the first place, to all those dispiriting reminders that "no means no"— pornography gives guys a world in which no one has to take no for an answer.

(pp. 174–175)

Therefore popular porn images create the illusion of complete power and control over women without fear of rejection or fear of sexual failure. They also become an exercise in revenge as discussed by Jensen (2007) and Dines (2010). Following interviews conducted by Kimmel (2008:182) with men who view porn, the following captures the mindset of many of them: "You don't have sex with women because you desire them: sex is the weapon by which you get even with them, or, even, humiliate them." He further adds:

They're not getting mad; they're vicariously getting even. Getting back at a world that deprives them of power and control, getting even with those haughty women who deny them sex even while they invite desire, getting back at the bitches and hos who, in the cosmology of Guyland, have all the power.

(p. 188)

In today's pornography, it seems that virtually no category of "women" is immune from attack. Indeed, there are particular body aesthetics at the center of mainstream porn that includes an overall firm/toned body, longer hair, make-up, shaved or waxed legs, vagina, anal area, and underarms. Race and age are also very important components in this "body aesthetics." White porn performers typically between the ages of 18 and 25 are desired. But, despite the popular, dominant images, many different categories of women have become the targets of the porn industry on some level.

Popular porn images prior to the late 1970s were often tied to the assumed "bad girls" in the sex industry (e.g., strippers), the entertainers, and the working class. But, Playboy began to change this image in 1979 when it published photographs of college women starting first with the publication of "Girls of the Ivy League." And, in the last decade, "The frequent visits of the *Girls Gone Wild* film crew to college campuses. . . . have also established an acceptance of porn chic norms on campus, leading more students to accept being photographed or captured on film in states of undress or nudity, accompanied by sexual content" (Lynch, 2012, p. 114). But, as stated above, many different categories of women today have been targeted by the porn industry: mothers, grandmothers, and even pregnant women, career and college women, younger and older, physically smaller and bigger women, and women of various racial and ethnic groups. The porn industry tries to ensure that no category of woman escapes its wrath in their pursuit to secure the message that any woman desires and/or deserves body-punishing sex and/or brutality. And, "In case the sexual acts alone aren't sufficient, the women in pornography constantly verbalize their status: '*I'm a cunt/slut/whore/dirty girl/etc.*' When women forget to say it, men remind them either with the question '*Are you a whore?*' or with the command '*Say you are a whore*'" (p. 116). On the other hand, "Most of the women outside pornography, the Madonnas, claim not to like to be treated that way sexually. But maybe, pornography suggests, just maybe those Madonnas are lying. Maybe deep down, all the Madonnas are really whores. Maybe they all like it like that—rough, painful, denigrating" (p. 117). Also, in addition to the label "whore," today's pornography commonly refers to women as "dirty," "nasty," and "filthy."

The production of racialized and racist images in porn has also become mainstreamed. For instance, Kimmel (2008) found that in addition to age, race and ethnicity also matter when it comes to pornography consumption. Almost none of the Asian-American men he spoke with, as well as Chicano men on the West Coast or in the Southwest expressed any significant interest in pornography. Latino men in the Northeast especially Puerto Rican and Dominican men, as well as African-American men across the United States indicated some interest but, small in relation to the consumption by white men. One of the most comprehensive studies done of sexual behavior in the United States (Laumann et al., 1994) found that the rates of masturbation among black men were about half the rates of white men. Kimmel notes that if we assume that one component of porn is to facilitate masturbation, then the lower rates of masturbation among black men may indicate lower rates of porn consumption.

Dines (2010) reminds us that: "The racial politics of the porn industry today mirror those of pop culture in that the majority of people involved in the production end of the business is white (p. 122). The genre that is typically marketed as "interracial" often features mainly black men with white women, and according to Adult Video News, this is one of the fastest growing and bootlegged genres in gonzo today. And, as Dines correctly observes, porn films and videos with other racial and ethnic combinations have different categories: for example, "Black" (which include black women performers), "Asian," "Latin," and "Ethnic." Since mainstream porn is typically produced by straight, white males for a predominantly straight, white male audience, women of color are generally depicted in gonzo films that have less status and less security.

As a result, the financial gains for black women are smaller. The desired jobs for porn performers are the ones that offer contract employment, and the two major porn-features studios, Vivid and Wicked, which offer such employment are reserved mostly for white women.

These studios, with their chic image, sophisticated marketing practices, and guarantee of regular work, afford their contract women an income and level of visibility that makes them the envy of the industry. (Jenna Jameson, of course, is held up as the quintessential example of just how far a contract porn star can go.) With surgically enhanced bodies, perfectly coiffed hair, and glamorous makeup, these women act as PR agents for the porn industry, showing up regularly on Howard Stern, E! Entertainment, or in the pages of *Maxim*. As the porn industry increasingly wiggles its way into pop culture, it is no surprise that it uses mainly white women as the "acceptable" face of porn; their all-American-girl looks seamlessly mesh with the blonde, blue-eyed images that grace screens, celebrity magazines, and billboards across North America.

(Dines, 2010, p. 123)

To date, there is little empirical research done on "interracial porn" but based on articles from Adult Video News it appears that porn films with white female and black male performers are in great demand by white porn consumers. As already mentioned, these are produced, marketed, and distributed primarily to a straight, white male audience. According to Dines (2010):

This seems strange given that a relatively short time ago, the thought of a black man just looking at a white woman was enough to work white men up into a lynch-mob frenzy. And now they are buying millions of dollars' worth of movies that show, in graphic detail, a black man doing just about everything that can be done to a white woman's body. But it is actually less strange when we realize that in the world of porn the more a woman—white or of color—is debased, the better the porn experience for the user. And what better way to debase a white woman, in the eyes of white men, than to have her penetrated over and over again by that which has been designated sexually perverse, savage, and debauched?

(p. 136)

Articles in *Adult Video News* and *XBIZ*, indicate that porn that includes both black male and black female performers are primarily targeted to a black audience and therefore there are less films and videos representing this genre given their smaller numbers in the larger U.S. population. On the other hand, there is a growing number of websites that depict sex between white men and black women, and the viewers appear to be white based on information posted on the various porn boards. "It seems that when either the male or female porn performer is white, then the audience is mainly white men" (p. 129).

Mainstream porn images remain racialized. Some include old racist themes about the enormously endowed and animalistic black man and the always sexually available animalistic black woman. Other examples include well-endowed black men with white women that appear more common and popular. These may serve as more evidence of "revenge porn" which was mentioned earlier; that is, white men's revenge against white women they can't have but using black men with bigger penises "as proxies to subordinate them" (Kimmel, 2008, p. 185). And as Dines notes, "In all-white porn, no one ever refers to the man's penis as 'a white cock' or the woman's vagina as 'white pussy,' but introduce a person of color, and suddenly all players have a racialized sexuality, where the race of the performer(s) is described in ways that make women a little 'sluttier' and the men more hypermasculinized" (p. 123).

Additionally, the content of online porn in online chat rooms needs to be more fully examined to gain deeper insight into the extent of porn use, as well as the desire for violent porn among straight men. For instance, Kimmel (2008) examined the content of porn in three different media: magazines, videos, and online chat rooms and found that violence increased in online chat rooms. The explicit violence was not because of technology but rather because the social context of the media changed. As Kimmel explains, magazines and videos are oriented towards individual consumption but online chat rooms are spaces where men can share porn and interact about the porn they view. "These chat rooms are the closest thing to a pornographic locker room, in which bonding is often accomplished by competing with the other guys. . . . The competition can become heated—and violent—rather quickly" (p. 187).

SUMMARY

Consumption of porn in the United States has steadily increased over the years (Maltz and Maltz, 2008; Paul, 2005; Sarracino and Scott, 2008) and, according to *Internet Pornography Statistics*, there are over 4 million pornographic websites (12 percent of total websites), and 68 million daily pornographic search engine requests which account for 25 percent of total requests. Also, 42.7 percent of all Internet users view pornography, and the average age of first Internet exposure to porn is 11 years of age. Overall, Internet pornography is a multi-billion dollar business and comprises approximately 12 percent of the Internet. But, it seems that the industry today cannot keep up with the demand by consumers for more porn overall, but, more specifically, more extreme porn that depicts outright brutality and degradation of women.

NOTES

1　See Stoltenberg, Joh (1994). *What makes pornography "sexy?"* Minneapolis, MN: Milkweed Editions; and Stoltenberg, John (1998). *The end of manhood: A book for men of conscience* (2nd ed.). Bridgewater, NJ: Replica Books.

2　For Corsianos, the expression of "sexual agency" requires that an individual be prepared and have the ability to critically evaluate sexual choices. This includes defining one's own sexual identity, and, making meaningful choices in terms of sexual acts that are free of coercion, rigid conformity to external social norms, or force.

Chapter 2

Adult Pornography Today

> Getting into porn is a death sentence.
>
> (Jameson, 2004, p. 386)

IT is often said that "the world is a different place today." Indeed, it is. It is a "post-*Playboy* world" (Jensen, 2007), one that features the degradation, abuse, and humiliation of women never seen before in the mass media. It is a world inundated with pornography. Translated from Greek, "pornography" means "writing about prostitutes" (Katz, 2006). Not to be confused with erotica, which is "sexually suggestive or arousing material that is free of sexism, racism, and homophobia and is respectful of all human beings and animals portrayed" (Russell, 1993, p. 3), many forms of pornography, on the other hand, hurt. Women are represented in many different ways in pornography, but two things that most mainstream pornographic images of and writings about them have in common is that they are characterized as subordinate to men and the primary role of female pornographic actresses is the provision of sex to men (Funk, 2006).

The focus of this book is on violent and demeaning images of women in mainstream pornography; that is, violent and degrading sexual materials that dominate the mass market and are readily available on Internet sites and other forms of media. Pornography has noticeably changed over the past few decades due to the Internet. Much, if not most, of the adult pornography easily accessible online is, as Gail Dines (2010), among many others, defines it, "gonzo—that genre which is . . . today one of the biggest moneymakers for the industry—which depicts hard core, body-punishing sex in which women are demeaned and debased" (p. xi). The intent here is not to moralize or to engage in "shock theater," but a typical example of "gonzo" pornography is warranted. Below is what Dines (2010), one of the world's leading experts on the subject, discovered while studying cyber porn:

> A few more clicks and I was at GagFactor.com owned by JM Productions, a much-talked-about site in the porn trade magazines. When I clicked on it I was invited to "Join us now to Access Complete Degradation." On the site were hundreds of pictures of young women with penises thrust deep into their throat.

Some are gagging, others crying, and virtually all have faces, especially their eyes, covered in semen. The user is bombarded with images of mascara running, hair being pulled, throats in a vicelike grip, nostrils being pinched so the women can't breath as the penis fills the mouth, and mouths that are distended by either hands pulling the lips apart or penises inserted sideways.

(pp. xix–xx)

Such images are part-and-parcel of today's Internet pornography. However, violent sexual images are easily accessible elsewhere. For instance, Bridges, Wosnitzer, Scharrer, Sun, and Liberman (2010) examined 304 scenes in 50 of the most popular pornographic DVDs and found that nearly 90 percent contained physical aggression (mainly spanking, gagging, and slapping) and roughly 50 percent included verbal aggression, primarily name-calling. Not surprisingly, males constituted most of the perpetrators and the targets of their physical and verbal aggression were "overwhelmingly female." Moreover, female targets often showed pleasure or responded neutrally to male aggression. To make matters worse, consider Brosi, Foubert, Bannon, and Yandell's (2011) empirically based observation:

[A]s the pornography industry grows and seeks to satisfy its increasingly large customer base, it has continuously innovated its products and materials in a direction of more extreme, violent, "edgy," material, often featuring underage actors and scenes depicting a wide variety of dehumanizing behaviors not heretofore seen.

(p. 27)

There are still many things we don't know about adult pornography and its negative effects, but Katz (2006) reminds us about one thing we do know for sure:

Mainstream pornography has changed a lot in the past couple of decades. People of a certain age who still associate heterosexual porn with "girlie magazines" and air-brushed photos of big-breasted women shot in soft light in luxurious beds with big pillows would be shocked by the brutality, outright contempt for women, and racism that is common in today's product.

(pp. 186–187)

While many women consume adult pornography, it is created primarily for generating sexual arousal in men (DeKeseredy and Olsson, 2011; Jensen, 2007; Corsianos, 2007). From the standpoint of many feminist scholars (e.g., DeKeseredy, 2009; Dworkin, 1994), pornography, regardless of whether it appears on the Internet, in stores, on television, in literature, or in other media, is also a variant of hate-motivated violence and it is now "normalized" or "mainstreamed" in North America and elsewhere (Boyle, 2010; Dines, 2010; Jensen, 2007), despite becoming more violent and racist (Boyle, 2010; Tankard Reist, 2009). For Melinda Tankard Reist (2009), "What was once considered unthinkable is now ordinary" (p. 11).

It is beyond the scope of this book to repeatedly describe the content on contemporary pornographic Internet sites, but some more brief examples of violence and racism are necessary. For instance, Doghouse Digital is a company that produced the video *Black Bros and White Ho's*, which offers stereotypical images of "the sexually primitive black male stud" (Jensen, 2007, p. 66). Another example is the interracial film, *Blacks on Blondes* featuring a white man in a cage, watching black men have sex with this wife (Dines, 2006). Additionally, there are thousands of other websites depicting women degraded and abused in a myriad of ways. Actually, a routine feature of new pornographic videos is painful anal penetration, as well as men slapping or choking women and/or pulling their hair while they penetrate them orally, vaginally, and anally (Bridges et al., 2010; DeKeseredy and Schwartz, 2013; Dines and Jenson, 2008).

The pornography, that is at the center of this book, not only hurts women porn "actors," but also the intimate female partners of the men who consume it. Many women report feeling betrayed, low self-esteem, anger, being pressured to imitate what their male partners had seen online, and a range of other negative effects that are not the result of physical force (Bridges and Jensen, 2011; Schneider, 2000). Male pornography consumption is also a powerful determinant of physical and sexual violence against current and former female partners (DeKeseredy and Schwartz, 2009, 2013), and it is strongly associated with attitudes supporting violence (Hald, Malamuth, and Yuen, 2010). Scientific evidence supporting these conclusions has improved considerably over the past 30 years. Before the early 1990s, however, there were limited data on how graphic sexual imagery influences men's violent behavior outside artificial laboratory settings. Hence, some critics argued that there is scant proof of any connections with "real world" behavior (Berger, Searles, and Cottle, 1991; Brannigan and Goldenberg, 1987).

Representations of the mainstreaming of violence against women in today's porn are evidenced throughout this book. Most feminists are undoubtedly aware of the gendered and racialized forms of violence and exploitation promoted by much of the adult porn industry, even as they oppose censorship, and advocate for protections for sex workers. Ariel Levy, in her acclaimed book *Female Chauvinist Pigs: Women and the Rise of Raunch Culture* (2005), warns against the increasing commodification of women's sexuality, and is critical of the porn-star aspirations of many teenage girls and young women, the growing popularity of breast enlargement surgeries and striptease aerobics, and is even critical of women "leaders" in the sex industry including Christie Hefner, the CEO of Playboy. For Levy, women have been conned into believing that sexual expression, regardless of its form, is their most important contribution.

But, regardless, there are also some feminist academics who find some value in all forms of pornography. For instance, queer feminists such as Jane Ward:

> make sexual self-determination and the pursuit of our own orgasms the highest goal when it comes to engaging porn. Lucky are those whose arousal results from homegrown and independently produced feminist porn cast with gender-

variant people of various races, body sizes, and abilities. But for some of us, mainstream porn—for all of its sexist and racist tropes and questionable labor practices—still casts its spell.

(p. 130)

But, what does it then mean for one to have a queer feminist relationship to porn? According to Ward (2013):

most efforts to answer this question presume that the answer lies in the means of production (Are films produced by and for women or queers? How are performers treated and compensated? Are all sex acts safe and consensual?) or in the virtual content of adult films themselves (Are we viewing genuine orgasms? What kind of bodies, desires, and subjectivities appear? Is the film directed and shot in a way that invites a queer and/or feminist gaze?).

(p. 130)

Also, academics such as George Washington University sociologist, Ronald Weitzer (2010) asserts that "pornography might contribute to the sex education of some or many viewers or . . . it might lead to mutually pleasurable sexual experiences for male and female viewers alike" (p. 667).[2] Susanna Paasonen (2010) states that some variants of pornography challenge what Weitzer refers to as "conventional power relations." Similarly, some feminists embrace the post-modernist view that pornography can be subversive and liberatory (Williams, 1989). As well, some sex-positive feminists contend that pornography is just as important to women as to men, and that there is nothing inherently degrading to women about such media (McElroy, 1995; Strossen, 2000). Peter Lehman (2006) is another example of a pro-porn scholar. He states, "If positions on pornography are staked out in this 'pro' or 'anti' fashion, I clearly come down on the side of pro-porn: I believe pornography can be complex, meaningful, and pleasurable and that it should be studied to enhance our understanding of sexuality and culture, not to fuel hysteria" (p. 20). For queer feminist Jane Ward (2013):

the beauty of queer desire is precisely that it is unpredictable, potentially unhinged from biological sex or even gender and as such, difficult to commodify. A given viewer may have a vagina, but while watching porn, who knows what kind of subjectivities emerge . . ., or what kind of imagery this viewer might enjoy. Sure, market research may indicate that women do, in fact, have group preferences (for deeper plot narratives, close-ups of female orgasms, and so on), but even these "feminist" preferences have been marketed to us, and arguably mirror simplistic cultural constructions of femininity, such as the notion that women's sexuality is more mental or emotional than physical.

(p. 135)

Queer, feminist and lesbian porn have attempted to reinvent new representations of desire and pleasure. For porn director Marit Ostberg (2010), "Feminist porn.

. . . wants to encourage people to feel sexy and to be sexual objects, but decide for themselves how, why, and for whom. Once you have that power it is much easier to decide when you DO NOT want to be sexual" (p. 103).

But, at the same time, queer feminist Ward (2013) recognizes that even though gender and desire are socially constructed, all porn is not politically-neutral, and there remains a fundamental need to critically evaluate what we consume.

Many younger women of the general population also find value in pornography (Attwood, 2005; Ciclitira, 2002; Hald and Malamuth, 2008). For some, this may be due in large part to "internalizing porn ideology, an ideology that often masquerades as advice on how to be hot, rebellious, and cool in order to attract (and hopefully keep) a man." In Corsianos (2007), some of the sexual behaviors described by self-defined "straight" college women was performed because it was "the thing to do to please your boyfriend," or, because it was "cool because the guys get a kick out of it" (p. 866).

Related to this problem is that scores of young women, especially North American female undergraduates, accuse some feminists of "denying them the free choice to embrace our hypersexualized porn culture" since as "rising members of the next generation's elite," they see "no limits or constraints on them as women" (Dines, 2010, p. 100). Consider what happened to Walter DeKeseredy in September 2007. Prior to this time, a southern Ontario university and another institution of higher learning located near it, had a 10-year history of allowing a "sex pub" on campus once a year. Described by its organization as an event designed "to promote awareness" and "safe sex," the "sex pub" in reality objectified women for the sake of profit and involved displays of pornographic pictures. According to one student who helped DeKeseredy cancel this pub night, "What you're doing is commodifying sex, so in other words, we can relate that to prostitution. So what are we saying to students? What are we saying about ourselves? What perception do we want to give out to students?" (cited in DeKeseredy, 2011a, p. 28). There was much student anger directed at DeKeseredy and this student, with much of it coming from women who claimed that they were stripped of their freedom to choose. Their protests were not in vain. Events similar to the "sex pub" have returned to these two schools. One, in particular, occurred on November 21, 2013 and was titled "Shirley's Dirty Bingo." As well, the Facebook advertisement for it states, "$1 per card, come be offended. Warning: this is VERY X-RATED."

THE PORNOGRAPHY BUSINESS

Millions of people around the world routinely consume gonzo and other types of pornography. In fact, men who do not consume pornography are atypical (DeKeseredy and Schwartz, 2013). Keep in mind that every second, over 30,000 Internet users view pornography (DeKeseredy and Olsson, 2011; Slayden, 2010), and the vast majority of them are men and boys (Dines, 2010). They, as Jensen (2007) states, are "not a deviation from the norm." Essentially, their means of obtaining sexual pleasure is, returning to Jensen, a result of "predatory corporate capitalism" (p. 17).

Pornography is "the quietest big business in the world" (Slayden, 2010, p. 57), and it is difficult to accurately determine the growth and value of this industry because its profits are not usually monitored through conventional business authorities (Maddison, 2004). What we can safely conclude, though, is that pornographers are the chief pioneers of new electronic technologies and they are closely linked with the development and success of video streaming, "tweeting," DVDs, 4G mobile phones, and broadband (Barss, 2010). Furthermore, many people watch sexual images at home by themselves and this market started to drive the home entertainment industry (Jordan, 2006), a transition that also influenced the viewing patterns of one of the common groups of pornography consumers: college fraternities (Foubert, Brosi, and Bannon, 2011; Kimmel, 2008).

Roughly 20 years ago, fraternity "brothers" went to pornographic theaters in groups. Some brothers interviewed by Sanday (1990) said that:

> seeing pornography is something to do before their parties start. They want to learn what it is like to "have a two foot dick" and to have a good time together. They never go alone, always together. They go together in order to have a good time, laugh, and make jokes during the movie. They dissociate themselves from the men who go alone to porno movies downtown and sit in seats "with coats and newspapers spread over their laps" and "jerk off" during the movie. They believe that this is sick, but they don't think "getting off" while reading *Playboy* privately or enacting a porno fantasy in their house is necessarily sick.
>
> (p. 129)

As mentioned earlier, we live in a post-*Playboy* world (Jensen, 2007) and pornography has moved from theaters to people's homes (as well as to their personal electronic devices), including those owned by fraternities. For example, in 2000, a man referred to by DePauw University fraternities as "The Smut Peddler" reported that he used to sell about 100 VHS pornographic tapes to the fraternities per year, but after 15 years in the "business," he witnessed a dramatic decline in sales due to Internet viewing (Claus, 2000). Fourteen years later, it is logical to assume that he has another "career" because of new technologies providing fraternity brothers easy and constant accessibility that cannot be offered by "Smut Peddlers."

Four years ago, there were over four million pornography sites on the Internet (Dines, 2010), with as many as 10,000 added every week since then (DeKeseredy and Schwartz, 2013). All of this is extremely profitable. Estimated worldwide pornography revenues from a variety of sources (e.g., Internet, sex shops, videos rented in hotel rooms, etc.) recently topped U.S.$97 billion. This is more than the combined revenues of Microsoft, Google, Amazon, eBay, Yahoo, Apple, Netflix, and Earthlink (DeKeseredy, in press; Zerbisias, 2008). More recent evidence of the growth of pornography is the emergence of online "tubes," such as YouPorn, XTube, and PornoTube, all modeled after the widely used and popular YouTube. YouPorn had 15 million users after launching in 2006 and was growing at a monthly rate of 37.5 percent (Mowlabocus, 2010; Slayden, 2010). What Schwartz and DeKeseredy (1997) stated 17 years ago still holds true today: rare are men who are not exposed to pornographic images. Even if people go out of their way to avoid pornography, it frequently "pops up" on people's computer monitors when they are working or "surfing the web" for information that has nothing to do with sex.

The relationship between sex and technology is not new. As Attwood (2010) reminds us, "technologies have always been adapted for sexual purposes, and it is regularly claimed that sex drives technological development" (p. 8). Still, what modern technologies do today is allow for pornography consumption to be part of what Attwood refers to as a "multitasking mode" involving users moving between "socializing, buying commodities, searching information, chatting, peeping, cruising, masturbating, and maintaining friendships" (Jacobs, 2004, p. 45). As well, webcam technologies enable a very large but unknown number of "amateur performers" to produce their own pornography at home and to profit from downloads of their videos. Note that amateurs who post their material on XTube receive 50 percent of the net profit for every download of their videos or photosets (Mowlabocus, 2010).

Pornography consumption is intensifying every day because of easy access offered by the Internet and large-scale, world-wide use of devices such as the iPhone and iPad. Also take into account that:

- Every second, U.S.$89.00 is spent on cyber porn.
- Sex is the most searched word on the Internet.
- Every day, 266 new pornography sites appear on the Internet.
- 35 percent of all Internet downloads are pornographic.

(Slayden, 2010, p. 54)

The exact accuracy of such claims is hard to ascertain, and they are sometimes contradictory. Even so, whether or not researchers ever obtain an absolutely accurate estimate of the percentage of males who consume adult cyber porn, most leading experts in the field agree with Robert Jensen's assertion that "It's become almost as common as comic books were for you and me" (Gillespie, 2008, p. A3). Chapter 1 provided a detailed description of the extent and distribution of pornography use and distribution, but some additional data are necessary here to support this claim. Consider that a national U.S. study of undergraduate and graduate students between ages 18 to 26 uncovered that 69 percent of the male and 10 percent of the female participants view pornography once a month (Carroll, Padilla-Walker, Nelson et al., 2008). Further, almost all Northern European boys have ever been exposed to pornography and 42 percent of Internet users between ages 10 to 17 in the United States had viewed cyber porn (Hammaren and Johnson, 2007; Mossige, Ainsaar, and Svedin, 2007; Wolak, Mitchell, and Finkelhor, 2007). A study done in Alberta, Canada found that one in three boys between ages 13 to 14 accessed sexually explicit media content on digital or satellite television, video and DVD, and on the Internet. More than one-third of the boys reported viewing pornography "too many times to count" and a sizeable minority of the boys in the sample planned social time around viewing porn with their male friends (Betowski, 2007). These are not innocent users who accidentally come across sexually explicit images, voices, and texts. Nor are they constantly bombarded with such material. Rather, they make a conscious effort to locate and choose to consume and distribute pornography (DeKeseredy and Schwartz, 2009, 2013). Unfortunately, data presented in Chapter 4 and elsewhere show that many consumers will commit criminal acts, including physically and sexually abusing their current or former intimate female partners.

The pornography industry is an "economic juggernaut" and numerous mainstream corporations, such as the Marriott, Westin, and Hilton hotel chains, accumulate huge profits from in-room porn movies. Some financial analysts report that these movies generate more money for these companies than revenue from hotel mini-bars. It should be noted in passing that, ironically, despite his public commitment to Mormon family values, former Republican Presidential candidate, Mitt Romney sits on the board of Marriott Hotels (Dines, 2010).

General Motors (GM), too, at one time made millions of dollars off pornography when it owned the U.S. national satellite distribution company DirecTV. GM sold its stake in DirecTV to Rupert Murdoch's News Corporation, but notwithstanding Mr. Murdoch's rabid conservatism (Manne, 2011), under his leadership, DirecTV continues to broadcast porn into "millions of American homes for a nice profit" (Frontline, 2013, p. 2). The list of other mainstream corporations profiting from porn is too long to provide here; however, a wealth of financial data reveal that this media has definitely "greased the rails" for large numbers of conventional businesses (Bennett, 2001; Slayden, 2010). As Lane (2001) observes, "pornography has been the World Wide Web's major economic success" (p. 34).

Mainstream pornography is lucrative for corporations and many producers, but it can often be cruel to many women porn performers, and they do not last long in the industry (Bridges and Jensen, 2011). The average employment period for "porn stars" only ranges from six months to three years and they often end their careers without money saved in the bank (Calvert and Richards, 2006). Certainly less than a handful end up becoming mainstream celebrities and *New York Times* best-selling writers like Jenna Jameson, author of the 2004 book *How to . . . Make Love Like a Porn Star: A Cautionary Tale*. It is also, as described in a previous section, not uncommon for women "actors" to be humiliated, degraded, and/or abused in the process of making cyber porn and other types of pornography. For the vast majority of women porn "actors," nothing could be further from the truth than Jameson's (2004) claim that "It's a good steady job, you make decent money, and despite everything we talked about, it's fun" (p. 387).

Porn consumers find almost anything that suits their fancy on the Internet. Once more, it is not our intent to engage in "shock theater," but Vargas-Cooper's (2011) observation is worth repeating here since much of what is described has now become "typical":

> groups of men—have sex with women who are seven months pregnant; the ho-hum of husbands filming their scrawny white wives having sex with paunchy black men in budget motels; simulations of father-daughter (or mother-daughter) incest; and of course, a fixture on any well-trafficked site: double anal.
>
> (p. 1)

True, as Vargas-Cooper points out, that human beings have had or desired what many would consider to be debased or criminal types of sex for centuries, but Internet porn now allows people to "flirt openly" with sexual acts that were always desired, but were long considered taboo, deviant, or against the law. And, any group of people is "ripe for the picking." Consider rural populations. Thousands of what DeKeseredy and Schwartz (2009) refer to as "the false images of rural life" are found on countless cyber porn sites. All one has to do is simply conduct a Google search using the words "rural gonzo porn." On September 11, 2012, DeKeseredy, Muzzatti, and Donnermeyer's (2013) hunt uncovered 108,000,000 results, with most of the videos being freely and easily accessible. Examples of the movie titles listed in their search are *Rural Discipline, Fuck Rural Milf, Raunchy Rural Granny Creamed, Rural SW Michigan Milfs, Rural Japanese Milfs, Rural Southern Wife Gets Ebony Cock*, and *Maturefarm*.

Contrary to what DeKeseredy et al. (2013) hypothesized, though, most of the gonzos they randomly examined did not feature big breasted, curvaceous farm girls like most of the women featured on the once popular U.S. variety television show *Hee Haw*.[3] Rather, a sizeable portion included submissive Asian women having sex in outdoor places. Despite this finding, one of the most popular U.S. female porn stars, Claudia Marie, often plays the stereotypical roles that we expected in rural gonzos and she is routinely subjected to painful "degradation ceremonies."[4]

Since their first search did not support their hypothesis, DeKeseredy et al. did another one to make sure that images of young women similar to those on *Hee Haw* are now at the margins. They were proved wrong after they typed the words "farm girl porn." Google reported 16,000,000 results on September 11, 2012 and major examples of film titles listed are *Two Outdoor Sluts Fuck Lucky Guy on Farm, Family Sex At the Farm, Sasha and Emma—Farmland Ass, Blake Mitchell—Farm Girl Fantasies, Big Tits Babe Fucked on the Farm*, and *Anal in the Farm*. Big breasts, halter tops, and frayed denim short-shorts are worn by most of the younger women in these movies and many are portrayed as farmers' daughters. Moreover, almost all of the sex acts take place outside or in barns. Similar images of women appear in thousands of farm Internet girl porn "comics" or "cartoons."

But, like many mainstream pornographic videos filmed in urban and suburban areas, the representations of women in rural porn are similar in that women are often represented as passive and as slavishly dependent upon men. The role of female characters is limited to the provision of sexual services to men. To the extent that women's sexual pleasure is represented at all, it is subordinated to that of men and is never an end itself as is the sexual pleasure of men. What pleases men is the use of their bodies to satisfy male desires. The sexual objectification of women is common to all pornography, in which women characters are killed, tortured, gang-raped, mutilated, bound, and otherwise abused, as a means of providing sexual stimulation or pleasure to the male characters (Longino, 1980, p. 42).

But, as stated earlier, it is difficult to find a group/category of "women" that has not been a target of abuse by the growing porn industry. "Women" of any shape, size, age, race, ethnicity, as well as, women who are urban, rural, college-educated, high school drop-outs, pregnant, menstruating, wealthy, poor, single, married, career women, and, stay-at-home moms have all been subjected to violent and demeaning attacks. But, at the same time, a disproportionate number are younger, white women who present particular body aesthetics (e.g., are often slim or athletic with long hair and makeup, and are without any body hair) (Corsianos, 2007).

In sum, pornography has moved in a few decades from a lucrative underground business with ties to organized crime to a huge corporate-capitalist industry that operates openly (Jensen, 2007). The swift growth of the Internet has also globalized access to violent and degrading pornographic materials on women and other potentially vulnerable groups in converged online and offline environments. Such media can be diffused to millions of people in only seconds due to faster ways of disseminating digital media productions, and the Internet facilitates access for those seeking pornographic content, whether it is legally recognized or not. What used to be rather difficult to access and a secret phenomenon is now accessible for larger groups and has subsequently become a huge business with operations around the world. The Internet not only facilitates access to previously inaccessible materials, but it also helps create an environment that normalizes hurtful sexuality and racism (Dines, 2010; Boyle, 2010; Tankard Reist, 2009).

THE PORNOGRAPHY EMPIRE STRIKES BACK: CHALLENGES TO CONFRONTING HURTFUL SEXUAL MEDIA

Though common images of today's mainstream pornography is degrading, racist, and violent, numerous citizens from all walks of life, especially pornographers and the millions who consume their products, argue that since an unknown but presumably large number of men who use cyber porn and/or other types of sexual media never abuse women, the assertion that porn is a key determinant of woman abuse is refuted. Yet, as Russell (1998) responds:

> This is comparable to arguing that since some cigarette smokers don't die of lung disease, there cannot be a causal relationship between smoking and lung cancer. Only members of the tobacco industry and some seriously addicted smokers consider this a valid argument.
>
> (p. 150)

Reputable studies reviewed in Chapter 4 show that many women are harmed or upset by their male partners' use of pornography. Based on reviewing data presented in that chapter, we could not agree more with Funk's interpretation of the empirical literature on the correlation between woman abuse and the pornography at the center of this book: "The research is quite clear: Not only does watching pornography decrease men's empathy for rape victims, but it also increases men's willingness to use force in their sexual acts" (p. 170).

Why is it that we have very firm reactions against seeing an animal beaten and raped but find it appropriate, or at least a free speech issue, to allow films approvingly showing women being tortured, raped, and beaten, as well as members of various ethnic groups (e.g., people of color, Latinos, etc.) depicted in ways that "sexualize racist stereotypes and violence" (Funk, 2006, p. 164)? We are not calling for censorship here because neither of us is in favor of it. However, we argue that in a better, equitable society, it would be considered morally reprehensible to show or promote certain types of sex films.

It is incorrect to assume, as many do, that all feminists are against pornography and want censorship. Rather, as stated earlier in this chapter, a variety of positions flourish. Obviously, many feminists want to eradicate porn, but there is also a strong feminist anticensorship position, such as that briefly described previously. Essentially, these authors believe that the evils to women of pornography are overstated. Actually, for a more extreme position, feminists informed by the writings of Ana Gronau (1985) contend that pornography, even its violent forms, should be freely available on college campuses and other public places (e.g., stores, theaters) because it is *functional* for women. For Gronau, pornography reminds women of the patriarchal forces that victimize and exploit them. If it is banned, then it is much more difficult for women to struggle against hidden patriarchy than it is to fight against the blatant and extreme forms of sexism found in pornography.

On the other hand, the pro-pornography works of Shimizu and Miller-Young on race in pornography attempt to challenge what they argue is the essentializing anti-porn feminist claim that porn is racist with no possibility for any kind of agency or critique from within or without. In her book, *A Taste for Brown Sugar: Black Women, Sex Work, and Pornography* (2014), Miller-Young attempts to capture the efforts of black porn performers to carve out space for creating sexual expression in ways that attempt to work within and against stereotypes. Similarly, in *At Home with Pornography: Women, Sex and Everyday Life* (1998), Jane Juffer examines the different material and discursive conditions in which different kinds of pornography are produced and consumed, and asserts that different representations of female pleasure must be expanded.

But, at the same time, regardless of the different porn genres available, it is necessary to remain critical of the dominant representations of violence and degradation against women in pornography today. Being critical of pornography, as we are, is not the same as advocating for censorship. On the contrary, as anti-porn activist, therapist, and educator Rus Funk (2006) puts it:

> Critiquing pornography, even critiquing pornography harshly, is not censorship. This behavior, in fact, is honoring freedom of speech. Furthermore, there have been more efforts to silence the voices of feminists who are critical of pornography, and the people who have been victimized in pornography, than there have been efforts by feminists or activists to shut down pornography.
>
> (p. 171)

Being critical of pornography is also necessary in examining what it means for women to have sexual agency. As Corsianos (2007) asks, can women experience sexual agency when they appropriate patriarchal definitions of sexual performances of female bodies as promoted in mainstream pornography? And, to what extent are consumers of porn performing learned behaviors of power politics rooted in patriarchal origins? These questions will be addressed in Chapter 5.

In mid-November 2014, Walter DeKeseredy gave a public lecture on violence against women in Canada to nearly 500 senior citizens belonging to a life-long learning group based in the Durham Region of Ontario, Canada. DeKeseredy's presentation featured a short section on the relationship between contemporary pornography and violence against women. He also briefly talked about the harm done to women "actors." To be expected, DeKeseredy was challenged on his critical views of pornography. Perhaps the best way of describing it is to quote Robert Jensen (2007) who asserts that the most common strategy people use to counter any criticism against porn is the trump card of "choice." "Because the women in pornography choose to perform, many argue, there can be no critique of the industry" (p. 82). The "choice" question was put to DeKeseredy by an elderly woman, which is surprising because it is usually men who use the "choice" and "choose" defense of pornography. Similarly, in Corsianos' popular *Pornography and Crime* classes, few students consider whether "choice" is meaningful and/or the result of free-will, and often students don't consider the socio-economic realities that lead some women to "choose" to work in the porn business.

The women and men who willfully participate in porn videos do have a choice, but it is structured. And, they are not "acting" (Funk, 2006). "Actors" are told what to do and the suffering they experience during scenes of degradation is real. Furthermore, Jensen (2007) is right to state that "free choices are rare" and that they are grounded in real-life conditions. For example, he and others (e.g., Baldwin, 1992) reveal that it is common for women porn "actors" to have a history of child sexual abuse that leads them to view their value in life primarily as the ability to sexually pleasure men. As well, many women in the industry are coerced into it by pimps, their boyfriends, and other men (Bridges and Jensen, 2011). Keep in mind Gail Dines' (2010) description of Jenna Jameson's childhood and early adulthood:

> Her mother died when she was two and her early life was chaotic, not least because she was at times neglected by her father. As a teenager, she was gang-raped, beaten, and left for dead and later raped by her abusive boyfriend's uncle. When she was sixteen, her father threw her out, so she went to live with her boyfriend, who encouraged her to start stripping. She was so desperate that in order to get her first gig, she removed her braces with a pair of pliers. Later on she became addicted to a cocktail of drugs and nearly died.
>
> (pp. 35–36)

Economic hardship is one more determinant of women's "choice" to enter the world of pornography. Compared to being "nickel and dimed" as a waitress or working in another part of the service sector (Ehrenreich, 2001), some women turn to pornography based on the perception perpetuated by Jenna Jameson and pornographers that the "money is good." The truth is that it isn't for most women in the industry. To repeat what was stated earlier, most women performers do not get wealthy and the industry "chew up and spits out women at an increasingly rapid pace" (Bridges and Jensen, 2011, p. 136).

Related to the claim of choice is the oft repeated assertion that porn is not a problem for women in the industry because they enjoy their work. Some men go as far to argue that women who do porn would perform even if they were not paid because of their intense desire for sex (Dines, 2010; Jensen, 2007). These myths are firmly entrenched in our society, especially among porn consumers and producers.

KEY LEGAL ISSUES IN PORNOGRAPHY

The topic of censorship was addressed in the previous section, but it is necessary to revisit it because there are also legal issues surrounding it.

In the United States, the Supreme Court has ruled that obscenity is not protected by the First Amendment, but the courts still need to determine what material is deemed obscene in each case. Material that is ruled obscene in accordance with the three-part test as set in the 1973 Supreme Court case of Miller vs. California is not constitutionally protected under the First Amendment. In Stanley vs. Georgia (1969) possessing obscene material, except child pornography, in one's own home is protected by the First Amendment, but it is illegal to post or transfer obscene material on the Internet. Also, distribution of obscenity is a criminal offense and often carries harsh penalties and prison sentences both at the federal and state levels. For instance, at the federal level, one who distributes obscene material may be fined and sentenced to a maximum of 5 years in prison for a first offense and additional offenses carry a 10-year maximum penalty.

Regulation of "obscenity" on the Internet is based on the current obscenity standard defined in Miller vs. California. There is no precise legal definition of obscenity. Courts rely on the test set forth by the Supreme Court in Miller vs. California to determine whether material is obscene. In Miller, the defendant was convicted for violating California's obscenity law by mailing unrequested sexually explicit material. The Court held that the state's interest in regulating obscene material was legitimate "when the mode of dissemination carries with it a significant danger of offending the sensibilities of unwilling recipients or of exposure to juveniles," such as sending material through the mail (Miller vs. California 1973). The Court outlined a three-part test to guide judges and juries in determining whether material was "obscene." Delivering the opinion of the court, Chief Justice Warren Burger wrote:

The basic guidelines for the trier of fact must be:

(a) whether the average person, applying contemporary community standards would find that the work, taken as a whole, appeals to the prurient interest;

(b) whether the work depicts or describes, in a patently offensive way, sexual conduct specifically defined by the applicable state law; and (c) whether the work taken as a whole, lacks serious literary, artistic, political, or scientific value.

Over the decades, the Supreme Court has refined the Miller test. It has approved the use of the Miller test to define obscenity at the federal level, and it has extended Miller to various modes of communication including the Internet. For example, if the obscene material crosses federal districts, then one can be prosecuted under federal obscenity laws (judges and jurors will use the Miller test to guide them in determining whether material was obscene). In Ashcroft vs. ACLU the Supreme Court addressed the applicability of the "local community standard" in determining whether material found on the Internet was obscene and the court upheld the "local community standard." Therefore, with regards to online material, using various local standards to judge obscenity requires the Internet publisher, in theory, to abide by the restrictions of the least tolerant community to minimize the risk of criminal prosecution. A single image may be found to be obscene in one geographic area but not in another, but once that image is posted to the Internet, anyone can access it across the country. Therefore, purveyors are subject to any community's standards.

EARLY ATTEMPTS TO REGULATE PORNOGRAPHY

Anti-pornographers MacKinnon and Dworkin defined pornography as the "graphic sexually explicit subordination of women whether in pictures or in words" (MacKinnon, 1993, p. 22). In the early 1980s, legislators in Minneapolis employed Dworkin and MacKinnon to draft a proposed new law that would define pornography as a human rights violation. The new law would recognize the violation of people's civil rights. Dworkin and MacKinnon argued that pornography is not "what it says" but rather "what it does"; in other words there were real consequences for women, which made pornography a form of sex discrimination. As a result of the new law, people who had been harmed by pornography could sue civilly. They could sue the directors, produces and/or distributors of pornographic material if they had been coerced into the making of pornography; forced to consume pornography; defamed by being used in pornography without consent; assaulted due to pornography; or subordinated as a member of a sex-based group through traffic in pornography. Other jurisdictions passed similar laws (e.g., Indianapolis, Los Angeles, and a number of cities in Massachusetts). Supporters of such ordinances criticized the opponents who claimed that these laws violated free speech. Supporters responded by saying that not everyone's "speech" was protected nor did everyone have freedom of speech; that is, multiple social hierarchies exist along, class, gender, race/ethnicity, sexuality lines which privilege some voices and silence or discredit others. MacKinnon has said that "before pornography became the pornographer's speech it was somebody's life." For MacKinnon and Dworkin, the U.S. Constitution protects freedom of speech, and pornographers are not restricted from the kinds of pornography they create.

But, their ordinance would punish those whose "speech" brought harm to others (Dworkin, 1994; MacKinnon, 1993).

During the Minneapolis hearings, before the new pornography laws were introduced, victims of pornography were for the first time given the opportunity to talk about the harmful role of pornography in their lives. According to MacKinnon, these hearings freed previously suppressed speech, and so would the ordinance. The Minneapolis hearings generated national publicity which led the federal government to revise the national commission on pornography. Attorney General William French Smith created the Attorney General's Commission on Obscenity and Pornography; they asked to hear from survivors of violent victimization and investigated the effects of violent as well as non-violent sexual materials. The Commission concluded that the "harms at which the ordinance is aimed are real and the need for a remedy for those harms is pressing." It concluded that "civil and other remedies ought to be available to those who have been in some way injured in the process of producing these materials." It also found that the civil rights approach would allow for the recognition of pornography as a form of sex discrimination and they included an entire chapter in their report on the harm done to pornography "actors"—the people who were directly involved but who had been virtually ignored in the past (MacKinnon, 1994; 1997).

But, ultimately, the Minneapolis ordinance and similar others were challenged and defeated. In 1985, the Seventh Circuit Court of Appeals held the ordinance unconstitutional on the grounds that it violated the First Amendment guarantees of freedom of speech, and in 1986 the Supreme Court declined to overrule the court's decision. For MacKinnon, if the material that is degrading and violent towards women is protected by the First Amendment, as the Seventh Circuit declared, these materials were still in violation of the Fourteenth Amendment that guarantees everyone equal protection under the law since pornography discriminates (MacKinnon, 1994; 1997).

In 1994, however, Congress adopted the "Violence Against Women Act" which contained a provision for a federal civil remedy to victims of gender-based acts of violence such as rape and assault even if no criminal charges had been filed against the perpetrator (42 U.S.C. § 13981). According to MacKinnon, "Congress made legally real its understanding that sexual violation is a practice of sex discrimination, the legal approach that the anti-pornography civil rights ordinance pioneered in legislative form."

But, unfortunately, in 2000, in a 5–4 decision, the Supreme Court invalidated this section of the Violence Against Women Act (United States vs. Morrison, 529 U.S. 598). Chief Justice Rehnquist, writing for the majority, held that Congress lacked authority, under either the Commerce Clause or the Fourteenth Amendment, to enact this section.

RECENT FEDERAL PROSECUTIONS OF OBSCENE PORNOGRAPHY

In 2000 and 2001, the LAPD began a number of investigations of pornographers on obscenity-related charges, but the terrorist attacks of 9/11 shifted both the administration's and police agencies' priorities to "fighting terror" rather than the porn industry. As a result, "On a local level, deals were struck. Those charged were let off with a slap on the wrist. And Porn Valley did what it does best—it went right back to business as usual" (Susannah Breslin, 2008). But regardless, the last decade did bring some federal obscenity prosecutions and convictions.

In 2003, Robert Zicari (aka Rob Black), Janet Romano (aka Lizzy Borden) and their company *Extreme Associates* were indicted by a federal grand jury in Pittsburgh on ten counts of the production and distribution by mail and the Internet of obscene pornographic materials. Zicari and Romano faced a maximum total sentence of 50 years in prison, a fine of $2,500,000, or both. Extreme Associates, Inc. faced a maximum total sentence of a term of probation of 50 years and a fine of $5,000,000. The prosecution also sought forfeiture of the films charged in the indictment, all gross profits from the distribution of the films, and all property used to facilitate the crimes, including the domain name extremeassociates.com. The company was well known for producing extreme violent pornography. During filming for a "PBS Frontline" documentary on obscenity, *American Porn*, (which aired on February 7, 2002), a PBS crew was repulsed by what they witnessed during filming and walked off the set of the *Extreme* movie, "Forced Entry" that graphically portrayed the beating, rape, and murder of women by a serial killer (based on the serial killer and serial rapist Richard Ramirez). The videos in the investigation included *Forced Entry; Ass Clowns 3*, which depicted a female journalist being raped by a gang led by Osama bin Laden; *Cocktails 2* that included scenes of women drinking vomit, and other bodily fluids; *Extreme Teen 24* that depicted a young girl being coached into having sex with an older man; and *1001 Ways to Eat My Jizz*. On January 20, 2005, District Court Judge Gary L. Lancaster dropped the charges. Part of the prosecution's argument was that the government had a legitimate interest in protecting adults from unwitting exposure to obscenity, and protecting children from exposure to obscenity. But, these arguments were rejected by the court, which also ruled that the federal obscenity laws were not narrow enough to meet these interests, and could not justify a complete ban on obscene material. According to Lancaster, children and unwitting adults are protected from the content because the website required a credit card to join, and because software was available for parents to restrict children's access to Internet pornography. But, by 2005, Alberto Gonzales, the new attorney general promised to reinstate a 10-count federal obscenity indictment against Zicari, Romano and their production company, and the Department of Justice announced the formation of the Obscenity Prosecution Task Force. By the end of the year, charges against Zicari and Romano had been reinstated. On March 11, 2009 Extreme Associates and its owners pled guilty to the reinstated obscenity charges to avoid trial, effectively shutting down the company. They were sentenced to one year and one day in prison, and *Extreme Associates* took its website down concurrent with the plea (Ward, 2009).

In June 2006, the U.S. Federal government in the district of Arizona brought a case against JM Productions of Chatsworth, California, its owners Jeff Steward and Mike Norton and distributor Five Star Video for distribution of obscenity (distributing the JM Production films). JM Productions produces and distributes films that are centered on the sexual degradation of women, violence and rough sex. For instance, in 2005 they released *Donkey Punch*, a film that consisted of four scenes in which men engage in rough sex with women, punching them repeatedly in the head and body throughout. In response to her experience on the set, Alex Divine said that "*Donkey Punch* was the most brutal, depressing, scary scene that I have ever done."[5] "Donkey Punch" is a slang term used to refer to a violent act that is committed during doggy-style sex, particularly anal sex that is falsely assumed to increase sexual pleasure for the penetrating partner. The practice involves the penetrating partner punching the receiving partner on the back of the head or in the lower back to make the receiving partner's anal or vaginal passage tense up, thus increasing the pleasure of the penetrative partner. Discussions centered on this urban legend appear to be popular on various pornography blog sites with little or no consideration given to the violent acts committed against the woman, including the fact that a blow to the head or neck can cause severe or lethal injury. Cyberspace Adult Video Reviews reported that due to the level of violence in the films they would no longer cover any further releases from JM[6]. The films since then appear to have been removed from the Internet.

By 2006, JM Productions received an 18-count federal obscenity indictment for "Gag Factor 15," "Gag Factor 18," "Filthy Things 6," and "American Bukkake 13." The case went to trial in 2007 in Phoenix, Arizona but at the first date of trial, the U.S. Department of Justice decided not to pursue the JM obscenity case any further due to lack of evidence that JM had sold the films to Five Star. But, District Court Judge Roslyn O. Silver proceeded with the case against Five Star Video and the company was ultimately found guilty of interstate transportation of obscene materials for sending a copy of "Gag Factor 18" to a FBI agent in Virginia, and sentenced to two years probation (*U.S. vs. Five Star Video, LC*; *U.S. vs. Five Star Video Outlet, LC*, 2007). The films in this case were directed by Jim Powers and depicted extreme acts of sexual degradation and rough sex. For instance, "Gag Factor" is a film series that features rough deep throating. Many scenes in the films have a woman hanging her head over the side of a bed or couch while a man repeatedly thrusts his penis down her throat. The "objective" is to make her gag until her face is covered with mucus, saliva, vomit and eventually semen. In the "American Bukkake" series typically 50–100 men will masturbate onto a woman.

Following the trial, Powers continued to direct "bukkake" films but also "gokkun" which included "American Gokkun 8." In bukkake, as mentioned above, the men masturbate onto the woman. In gokkun, men ejaculate into a container for the receiver to drink. In "American Gokkun 8," a 25-year old woman named Ami Emerson who, according to Susannah Breslin (2008) got into porn to pay off her student loans, eats 71 men's semen, which had been mixed into an omelet.

In 2007, both Ira Isaacs and Paul Little were indicted on obscenity charges. Ira Isaacs, an LA-based producer and distributor of scat and bestiality videos was indicted on obscenity charges. By 2013, Isaacs was sentenced to 4 years in prison for violating federal obscenity laws for four videos that showed scatology and bestiality and the women appeared drugged. Isaacs had previously cited "2 Girls 1 Cup" as inspiration that poop porn could become widely popular[7]. The video

"2 girls 1 cup" originated from a Brazilian distributor and pornographer Marco Antônio Fiorito. Some of Fiorito's films were viewed as violating obscenity laws; they depicted bukkake, fisting, and depictions of defecation, urination, and vomiting in conjunction with various sex acts. Federal prosecutors filed criminal charges against Danilo Croce, a Brazilian lawyer living in Florida who was listed as an officer of a company distributing Fiorito's films in the United States. Croce was charged with accepting Internet payment for obscene materials, then shipping those obscene materials through the mail. In the end, Croce accepted a plea bargain and was sentenced to three years of unsupervised probation and forfeiture of $98,000 (Department of Justice, 2007).

Paul Little (aka Max Hardcore) and his company Max World Entertainment, Inc., were indicted by the U.S. Department of Justice with five counts of transporting obscene material by use of an interactive computer service and five counts of mailing obscene material relating to five movies that showed fisting, urination, and aggressive oral sex. And, in 2008, a Tampa jury found Little guilty on ten counts of federal obscenity charges and he was sentenced to 46 months in prison. The jury also ordered the Internet domain www.MaxHardcore.com to be forfeited (Montgomery, 2008). Little is recognized in the industry as one of the "founders of gonzo." Many of his films are centered on the degradation and humiliation of women who are depicted as underage girls and who are vaginally penetrated with speculums, urinated on by Little, and have forced aggressive oral sex where Little repeatedly shoves his penis down their throats to the point where they gag, gasp for breath and throw up.

On the other hand, Evil Angel and its owner Stagliano (also known in the industry as "The Buttman"), were indicted in 2008 on federal obscenity charges by a federal grand jury in Washington, DC. But, in 2010, as the federal trial began, all charges against Stagliano were dismissed due to insufficient evidence linking him to the production and distribution of two DVD videos (Hsu, 2010). Many of his films include deep throating, rimming, ass-to-mouth, spanking, domination, toys including various butt plugs, nipple clips, anal beads, dildos and vibrators, and also include the spreading open of the woman's anus or vagina in between acts of penetration, spitting on genitals and in women's faces, as well as, grabbing of the women's heads and throats.

GIVEN THE MILLIONS OF ONLINE PORN SITES, WHY ARE THERE SO FEW PROSECUTIONS? ARE THE POLICE INVESTIGATING VIOLENT ADULT PORNOGRAPHY?

When police resources are dedicated to policing pornography, they are often focused on investigating child pornography. In current research being done by Corsianos, detectives have described investigations regarding child pornographic material as priority investigations particularly if the victim is known (i.e., identified by someone in community) and the police suspect a family member, or neighbor in the production of child pornography. Typically, the police want to move quickly to ensure the child is saved and to prevent other children from becoming victims. The police will download the material and get a subpoena that is issued for the IP address. Once they have the address they can then obtain a search warrant to search the residence and seize all digital media. If the address is not in their jurisdiction, they contact the relevant police agency in the area, as well as, the FBI to investigate.

Violent pornographic images of women, on the other hand, are not prioritized. Detectives note that complaints from citizens regarding this kind of material are less common, and therefore, any police work in these kinds of investigations is reactive rather than proactive where the police would take the initiative to identify possible crimes. Also from discussions between Corsianos and detectives to date, it appears that police don't give much thought to whether these materials may be "obscene" and therefore criminal. Rather, detectives often stress the difficulty in determining whether the women in the videos are "performing" or, assume that they have given "consent" to the violent acts committed against them. But when investigating any assault (stranger or domestic), the job of the police is to determine whether there is "probable cause"; that is, if there's evidence to suggest that an assault has occurred then an arrest must be made. Officers do not ask alleged victims if they consented to the assault. Consent to being assaulted/abused is irrelevant. For instance, if an officer observes one person beating another on the street, the assailant will be arrested and charged with assault regardless of whether the victim says "I gave him permission to do this." But, in violent pornography, for example, detectives appear to view the women as "consenting" to the violence. In the police-observed assault example above, someone is harmed as in the pornography example. But, in the former instance, police recognize that one cannot consent to the assault. However, the opposite appears to be true in violent pornography cases. To the disapproval of the National Coalition for Sexual Freedom, to date there doesn't appear to be a single appellate court decision in the United States that has accepted consent as a defense in an assault or abuse prosecution arising from violent sexual behavior including BDSM conduct (NCSF.org).

Detectives assume that all women in pornography are consenting because they appear to be participating. They don't question whether the women were forced or coerced into it; or whether they were given partial information of what they would experience. For instance, in the PBS documentary discussed earlier, the woman featured in "Forced Entry" was told she would be "roughed up a little" but she was not told the extent of the brutality she would experience. One has to wonder how often women may be agreeing to certain conditions but in the process of making the film/video they find themselves in very different situations where they are fearful of stopping and/or are coerced to "go along with it."

Definitions of assault and abuse are defined by state laws. It should be noted though that there are state statutes that provide for consent as a defense but only in specific circumstances where, for instance, injury is not serious, or injury is a reasonable foreseeable hazard as in the participation of a particular sport. Many such laws follow the language of the Model Penal Code's (MPC) section on consent. According to MPC section 2.11(2) Consent to Bodily Injury:

> When conduct is charged to constitute an offense because it causes or threatens bodily injury, consent to such conduct or to the infliction of such injury is a defense if:
>
> a. the bodily injury consented to or threatened by the conduct consented to is not serious; or
> b. the conduct and the injury are reasonable foreseeable hazards of joint participation in a lawful athletic contest or competitive sport or other concerted activity not forbidden by law.

Also, with respect to who cannot give consent, many such laws resemble the language of the Model Penal Code Section 3. Consent cannot be given if:

> a. it is given by a person who is legally incompetent to authorize the conduct charged to constitute the offense; or
> b. it is given by a person who by reason of youth, mental disease or defect or intoxication is manifestly unable or known by the actor to be unable to make a reasonable judgment as to the nature or harmfulness of the conduct charged to constitute the offense; or
> c. it is given by a person whose improvident consent is sought to be prevented by the law defining the offense; or
> d. it is induced by force, duress, or deception of a kind sought to be prevented by the law defining the offense.

And, as mentioned above, there doesn't appear to be a single appellate court decision in the United States that has accepted consent as a defense in an assault or abuse prosecution arising from violent sexual behavior.

Police attempts to locate the women in pornographic videos and films where violent acts are committed against them, are not considered by law enforcement even though, according to federal obscenity laws, producers of porn that show sexual activity must maintain records of the names and ages of the "performers" and make them available to the Department of Justice upon request. Due to budget constraints, limited resources and an overall reluctance to recognize or consider crimes in adult pornography, most police work in this area, as noted above, is reactive. When police do investigate, typically it's in response to public complaints about a particular website, or Internet service provider that is hosting offensive material and/or allows illegal activities to occur on sites.

However, having a designated detective unit such as a specialized Computer Crimes unit, or, an Obscenity Crimes unit is the key to identifying some of these crimes. For example, one study that investigated the prevalence of online child pornography production investigations and arrests by U.S. law enforcement agencies, as well as the training and resources dedicated to investigating cybercrimes (Marcum,

Higgins, Ricketts, and Freiburger, 2011), found that specialized task forces and an increased number of sworn officers in a law enforcement agency increased the number of production of child porn investigations and arrests in a jurisdiction. Out of the 168 agencies surveyed serving populations over 50,000, 30 percent had designated task forces for cybercrimes and 41 percent had received general cybercrime training.

But, police resources overall are concentrated on fighting street crimes (e.g., drug crimes). Obscenity crimes committed on the Internet, as well as the physical and sexual assaults of pornography "actors" are relegated to the margins. Cybercrimes do not occur in a physical setting and yet most law enforcement training is focused on enforcing street crimes. "Due to the increasing prevalence of cybercrimes in recent years, some law enforcement agencies are attempting to address this with additional resources" (Broadhurst, 2006; Hinduja, 2004). The digital crime scene crosses county, state or international lines (Katos and Bednar, 2008). Since the mid-1990s some police agencies have developed CERTs (computer emergency response teams) to investigate public complaints as well as search for Internet service providers who are hosting material believed to be obscene (Broadhurst, 2006). But, requiring all police agencies to have a specialized cyber obscenity crime units with ongoing training for their officers and ongoing collaborations with other agencies are necessary in taking a stand on violence against women; prioritizing these crimes is a necessary step in combating the mainstreaming of these types of crimes. For instance, the FBI's Innocent Images project requires the FBI to collaborate with multiple other agencies in their efforts to decrease child pornography and exploitation online (FBI, 2011). As a result of this initiative, between 1996 and 2007, there was a 2062 percent increase in the number of cases opened, and a 1401 percent increase in the number of arrests (FBI, 2011).

Also, law enforcement has largely failed to consider the possibility that adult violent pornography can be investigated as possible "hate crimes" when they represent misogynous acts against women. Currently, forty five states and the federal government have enacted legislation that increases punishment for those convicted of a "hate crime." Hate crimes are committed against individuals by an offender motivated by hatred toward the victim's race, ethnicity/ancestry, gender identity, sexual orientation, religion, or physical disability, real or perceived. But, states differ on which identity categories are included in their hate crime legislation. Hate crime legislation allows the courts to consider the perpetrators' thoughts/psyche and "speech" to determine "hatred" for a particular group and then increase punishment if convicted. Supporters of hate crime legislation assert that people can think what they want, even hate who they want, but when they act to harm someone because of their hatred towards the person's gender, race, etc. (real or perceived) then punishment should be increased given the larger societal consequences of these crimes. Supporters of this approach argue that pornographers who produce misogynistic films that harm women "actors" are "acting out" their hate speech and thus have committed hate crimes. But, this at the moment does not appear to be law enforcement's understanding of hate crimes.

SUMMARY

This book is not about pictures, words, and movies that have a minimal impact on people. Instead, it is about media that hurt human beings, primarily women, on a variety of levels. Internet and other types of porn are already so brutal that it is hard to imagine that violent images, as well as their negative effects, could get worse. However, the future looks bleak because, as demonstrated in this chapter, so much money is being made by pushing the cruelty line (Jensen, 2007). The fact that harmful cyber porn and other types of pornography constitute a multibillion dollar industry reveals that our media, politicians, and society in general do not find violent and degrading images of mostly women problematic. As is often said, "What's wrong with this picture?"

DISCUSSION QUESTIONS

1. What are possible explanations to the increasing images of violence against women in porn today?
2. Why are people reluctant to think critically about today's online sexual media and assume that women's "choices" to be in the porn business are necessarily meaningful?
3. Why do you think there are so few obscenity prosecutions in the United States?
4. Why is law enforcement reluctant to investigate violent, adult pornography?

NOTES

1. Also see Flood's (2010) review of studies of the educational and "healthy" effects of viewing pornography.
2. *Hee Haw* featured country music and humor. CBS aired it from 1969 to 1971 and then it had a 20-year run in local syndication.
3. U.S. sociologist Harold Garfinkle (1956) coined the term "degradation ceremony." He states, "Any communicative work between persons, whereby the public identity of an actor is transformed into something looked on as lower in the local scheme of social types, will be called a 'status degradation ceremony'" (p. 420).
4. See http://ExtremeGirlForum
5. See Cyberspace Adult Video Reviews (September 12, 2005), retrieved September 8, 2013.
6. See www.trutv.com/library/crime/blog/2013/01/17/two-girls-one-cup-creator-gets-4-years-for-obscenity/index.html.

Chapter 3

Thinking Theoretically About Pornography

> The men who make the pornography have a good idea what their viewers want. Over and over again, they describe a male consumer who is angry, sexually frustrated, and eager to exact some revenge on women.
>
> (Kimmel, 2008, p. 187)

W HY does violent and abusive pornography exist? The answer to this question is obvious: there is a large market for it and it grows bigger every day. Yet, males are not hard-wired to consume gonzo and other porn. Nor are the vast majority of men and boys who view and read violent porn mentally ill or "sick." Consider the extent of porn consumption described in Chapters 1 and 2. If only a handful of men in the United States, Canada, the United Kingdom, and elsewhere routinely watched and/or read hurtful sexual media, it would be easy to accept non-sociological accounts of their behavior: they must be disturbed individuals. Not to belabor the point, but unfortunately, like violence against women, pornography is deeply entrenched in our society. Certainly, as Lehman (2006) puts it, how could pornography be "such a big business if only some 'perverts' whom nobody knows but everyone imagines exist out there somewhere used it?" (pp. 10–11). The main objective of this chapter, then, is to review sociological answers to two questions: why do men consume violent porn and what are the effects of their consumption? However, since there are competing psychological explanations for why people consume hurtful porn, it is first necessary to briefly describe and critique a few recent individualistic accounts.

PSYCHOLOGICAL THEORIES[1]

Social scientific theories of pornography use and its effects are not as plentiful as those of other social problems, such as murder, poverty, and unemployment. This is because pornography is still considered by many scholars and university/college administrators as a topic unfit for academic inquiry (Ullen, 2014). Undoubtedly, you would be hard pressed to find courses on pornography in the majority of institutions of higher learning scattered across North America and elsewhere. Nonetheless, this book is one of an increasing number of texts and scholarly monographs on hurtful sexual media that have been produced over the past several decades, and a growing number of academics now provide sophisticated scholarly answers to the question "[W]hy would anyone with a Ph.D. in an established discipline research and teach a valueless, meaningless form that appeals to the prurient interests of presumably abnormal people, or perverts as they are commonly called?" (Lehman, 2006, p. 4).

For reasons provided in the first two chapters and in other sources, "pornography requires our interpretation" (Kipnis, 1996, p. 62). Nonetheless, there are different scholarly understandings, with psychologists mainly linking individual factors to porn use. One such psychological offering contends that antisocial personality characteristics motivate some people to seek out Internet pornography. According to this account:

> The "goodness of fit" of antisocial personality characteristics with antisocial sexual content will, it is speculated, promote a tremendous depth of involvement in antisocial sexual stimuli. Individuals may lose awareness of the constraints of reality regarding enactment of antisocial sexual behavior.
>
> (Fisher and Barak, 2001, p. 312)

A related theory is that normal-range people will avoid antisocial, sexually explicit material and will reject such media's messages if encountered (Fisher and Barak, 2001). The truth is, though, that pornography consumers are "less pathological than expected" (Gondolf, 1999, p. 1). Based on a review of the survey data on porn consumption patterns, it could easily be argued that men who do not consume porn are not "normal-range people." Note, too, that the survey data reported previously *underestimate* porn consumption. There are many reasons why porn users might not disclose their consumption. Some people are embarrassed to reveal their experiences. As well, methodologists often worry about forward and backward telescoping. Here a person who has used porn often might be unable to accurately place each time he or she did so in a specific time period, such as when asked how often something happened in the past 6 months. Anyone who has ever felt that a series of events all ran together in their mind would understand this problem. There is also simple memory error: people could just plain forget about viewing or reading porn. Then, of course, there is also purposeful deception (DeKeseredy and Schwartz, 1998a; Meloy and Miller, 2011; Schwartz, 2000).

New technologies have plusses and minuses. For example, advances in technology make it easier than ever before for researchers who collect survey data to interview a random sample of people who own landline telephones. Yet, this is also the problem. More and more people, and especially younger ones, only have cell phones and cannot be interviewed on landlines. Others without access to landlines might also be low-income people, homeless people, and persons who are in mental health institutions or prisons. There are other problems that contribute to under-reporting (e.g., language barriers) and all of them are difficult to overcome and are not likely to be eliminated in the future (DeKeseredy and Schwartz, 2013).

That an ever-growing number of people consume porn nullifies the above second psychological perspective reviewed here. As well, there is little support for the *imitation model* (Bridges and Jensen, 2011; Silbert and Pines, 1984), a parsimonious theory that asserts people imitate behaviors they see in the media. The relationship between media exposure and people's actions is much more complex. Albeit highly popular in journalistic and political arenas, the so-called "copycat effect" is nowhere near as widespread as people think. Also, the bulk of the data supporting the imitation model are derived from laboratory studies in which researchers attempt to strip away dozens of influences on human behavior and isolate exactly what they want to study. However, in the real world, we live and operate under the influence of all these confusing factors. What happens when we step out of the laboratory and return to real life? As Jensen (2007) observes, "The complexity of confounding variables and the imprecision of variables makes these studies virtually useless" (p. 103). To the best of our knowledge, no studies have been conducted to date conclusively showing that people's laboratory behavior is consistent with their conduct in the community.

There are other more complex psychological theories, such as the social learning, sexual script, and other cognitive models reviewed and critiqued by Bridges and Jensen (2011). What is missing from these accounts and other psychological offerings is what the late C. Wright Mills (1959) refers to as the "sociological imagination." This is hardly a trivial concern, given that there is no reliable evidence linking personality disorders, biological factors, or alcohol/drug abuse to cyber porn use (DeKeseredy and Olsson, 2011; Stack, Wasserman, and Kern, 2004). Similarly, less than 10 percent of all incidents of intimate violence result from mental disorders (DeKeseredy, 2011a; Gelles and Straus, 1988). Of course, it is incorrect to completely reject individualistic explanations. These points of view, to a certain extent, do help us make sense of criminal or deviant acts committed by *some* people. For instance, for some people, psychological factors can influence their decision to assault women or to view degrading, violent pornography. Further, some people are stopped from committing future crimes through the use of therapy, psychotropic drugs, and other psychologically and biologically informed treatments.

SOCIOLOGICAL THEORIES[2]

Sociological theories reviewed here range from conservative accounts to progressive explanations, but what they all have in common is the aforementioned sociological imagination. This perspective calls for an understanding of how *personal troubles* are related to *public issues*. Personal troubles are just what you might think. If you are raped, robbed, beaten, or cheated, you have a problem and you have to deal with it. You may need medical attention, comfort from friends or family, financial help, or some other type of social support. Sometimes, however, many people are suffering individually from the same personal problem at the same time. If 100 women are sexually assaulted in one year on one North American college campus, each one of these women has a personal problem or personal trouble. At the same time, though, something about the broader structural and cultural forces, such as patriarchy or capitalism, Mills (1959) would argue, allows for so very many women to be harmed. To be able to look beyond the personal troubles of one or two female students who have been sexually assaulted and see the broader problem of rape on campus and its causes is to possess the sociological imagination.

Consider male-to-female violence in private places. At first glance, a man who beats the woman he shares an intimate relationship with apparently must be either suffering from life-events stress or be mentally ill. Perhaps that seems an adequate explanation for the two or three cases you know well. Yet, when you begin to look at the 11 percent or so of women in North American marital/cohabiting relationships who are physically abused annually by their male partners (DeKeseredy and Schwartz, 2013), you begin to find "an indication of a structural issue having to do with the institutions of marriage and the family and other institutions that bear upon them" (Mills, 1959, p. 9). Now that we have provided a rationale for analyzing pornography use and its effects sociologically, we can go ahead and review some sociological perspectives that have had a major impact on a modern social scientific understanding of pornography.

STRUCTURAL FUNCTIONALISM

Emile Durkheim is one of sociology's greatest thinkers and deemed by many social scientists to be the founder of *structural functionalism*, a school of thought that informs, to the best of our knowledge, the first sociological theory of pornography to be crafted. Developed by Ned Polsky (1969), prior to reviewing this perspective, it is first necessary to briefly summarize Durkheim's four major sociological ideas.

First, Durkheim viewed human beings as innately egoistic. Compared to animals, they are not satiated when they fulfill their biological needs. According to Durkheim (1951), "The more one has, the more one wants, since satisfactions received only stimulate instead of filling needs" (p. 248). Since people cannot control their desires by themselves, they must be held in check by external forms of social control. Society must control people's rampant egoism by acting as a "regulative force [that] must play the same role for moral needs which the organism plays for physical needs" (1951, p. 248). Without such control, many people are likely to rob, beat, and kill one another to satisfy their ever-increasing financial and psychological desires. In his interpretation of Durkheim's call for external control, Desmond Ellis (1987) asks us to imagine what society would be like if it was composed solely of "infants whose every psychological and material want must be continuously satisfied without regard to the wants of others" (p. 28).

Second, Durkheim argued that social order is based on value consensus. All of us are assumed to believe that it is wrong to beat, kill, and rob others. These values are learned and preserved through interaction with others who advocate them.

Third, sports, religion, corporations, crime, schools, and so on exist in our society because they are *functional*. In other words, these phenomena and institutions exist and will continue to exist because they have a function: they benefit society as a whole.

Finally, because Durkheim was what sociologists term a *structural functionalist*, he viewed society as similar to a biological organism. In a perfectly working human body, all the parts work together to provide good health. A great body with broken-down kidneys is in deep trouble. In the same way, society consists of many interdependent parts that operate to give it equilibrium. In North American society, structural functionalist argue, families, schools, criminal justice systems, places of worship, and other institutions all help to maintain a balanced social system. Although a change in one or more of these parts will change the others, the direction of change is usually toward restoring equilibrium or dealing with the disturbances caused by social change.

Included among the best known contemporary sociological examples of the use of structural functionalist theory to interpret recurring types of social problems is Polsky's (1969) theory of pornography. The starting point for his perspective is this dated paradoxical finding: at the time in which he crafted his offering, in most societies in which it existed, pornography was widely regarded as a stigmatized, illegitimate form of sexual expression. How, then, could it continue to exist when it was condemned? The answer is, according to Polsky, that pornography performs an important function for society by permitting the expression of antisocial or illegitimate sex.

Polsky's functionalist argument is clearly distinct from that offered by feminist scholar Anna Gronau (see Chapter 2) and proceeds as follows. Men's sexual urges are not inherently social. Rather, they cater to individual satisfaction. Left to themselves, men would flit from one woman to the next, and with each, they would engage in a myriad of sexual acts that would produce pleasure for them, but not necessarily children for society. Children mean responsibilities, and responsibly cared for children ensure the continuance of society. If children are properly socialized, something has to be done about regulating man's egotistical sexual inclinations.

The solution is to connect sexual inclinations and social and family respons-ibilities by making a broad distinction between what is deemed typically "legitimate" and "illegitimate sex." Legitimate sex is confined to a married partner and (within marriage) to sexual activities that are most likely to lead to procreation. But man's quest for novel sexual experiences remains as strong as ever. These illegitimate forms of sex also need to be expressed. They help "drain off" antisocial urges, and in this way enable men to bear the social burdens imposed on them by confining illegitimate sex to the "missionary position" with a married partner. So, for Polsky, pornography offers vicarious enjoyment of various kinds of forbidden but desired sexual activities. In sum, pornography is functional for society because, by permitting the expression of "antisocial sex," it acts as a safety valve and thus keeps families together.

Polsky's work is, again, dated. Hence, it does not take into account the content of today's porn, the current widespread acceptance of it, and the negative consequences of consuming hurtful porn. Needless to say, too, some scholars sharply fault Polsky for viewing men's sexual desires as being "natural," contending that their sexual appetites are learned. Related to this criticism is another one that views Polsky's work as too biological, as is often said about Durkheim's writings (Taylor, Walton, and Young, 1973). Not surprisingly, too, feminists assert that rather than ameliorate social problems, pornography exacerbates them, which is a central theme of this book. Actually, as pointed out in Chapter 2 and elsewhere, many women married to men who consume pornography do not view such media as a safety valve. Recall that numerous women with partners who consume porn report feeling betrayed, low self-esteem, anger, being pressured to imitate what their male partners had seen online, and other negative effects, such as violence. As well, Shope (2004) found that a male partner's pornography use doubled the risk of a battered woman being sexually assaulted and more will be said about violence against women and porn in Chapter 4. Additional negative effects on interpersonal relationships, such as marriage include increasing negative attitudes toward women, blunted affect, and an increase in dominating behaviors (Bridges and Jensen, 2011).

Keep in mind, too, that rather than keep families together, some studies show that porn is a major correlate of between two-thirds to 56 percent of divorces in the United States (Manning, 2004; Skinner, 2011). For reasons presented here, if pornography is functional, then it primarily benefits those who produce it because not only does porn hurt women, but it also damages scores of men who use it. Gail Dines (2010) provides a few examples derived from her conversations with some members of a rapidly growing group of college men who are addicted to porn:

> Some of the worst stories I hear are from men who have become so desensitized that they have started using harder porn and end up masturbating to images that previously disgusted them. Many of these men are deeply ashamed and frightened and they don't know where it will all end. Phil told me, "Sometimes I can't believe the porn I like. I feel like a freak," and Anthony sees it as a "slippery slope I never thought I would slide down. I never thought of myself as a guy who would like the really hard-core porn, but that's what happened to me." Some speak of moving toward more violent images while others have become increasingly interested in bondage and even child porn.

(pp. 93–94)

AN INTEGRATED SOCIAL BOND THEORY OF INTERNET PORNOGRAPHY USE

Fast forwarding from 1969 to the start of this new millennium, Stack, Wasserman, and Kern (2004) offer a "blended theoretical perspective" that combines elements of social control and opportunity theories of deviance. The foundation of their offering is Travis Hirschi's (1969) social bond theory. Following Thomas Hobbes (1963), a conservative seventeenth century English philosopher who devoted a substantial amount of his intellectual energy to addressing the issues of social order and social control, Hirschi argued that all human beings are naturally inclined to commit crimes and deviant acts. But, why, then, do most people obey the law and engage in conforming behavior? His answer to this question is that an individual's strong *social bond* to conventional society stops him or her from being deviant and breaking the law. Stated in reverse, "delinquent acts result when an individual's bond to society is weak or broken" (p. 16). The elements of the social bond empirically examined by Stack et al. using 2000 General Social Survey data are: marital, religious, socioeconomic, and bonds to conservative or liberal beliefs.

The opportunity theory embedded in Stack et al.'s account is heavily driven by Cohen and Felson's (1979) routine activities theory of predatory street crime. Since it was first developed by these criminologists, routine activities theory has been widely cited, discussed, and tested. It remains one of the most popular mainstream criminological approaches although it has succeeded only partially at one of its original goals, namely deflecting attention from offenders' motivation. This lack of concern has been one of the primary criticisms of the theory. Virtually all of those who use it have built motivation back in.

The key part of routine activities theory is that the amount and location of crime affected, if not caused, by three important factors: the presence of likely offenders, who are presumed to be motivated to commit the crimes; the absence of effective guardians; and the availability of suitable targets (Cohen and Felson, 1979). Although this point is rarely discussed, an important element of this theory is that there must be offenders who are likely to commit crimes if they have the opportunity to do so. All commentators refer to this factor as "motivated offenders," but Felson reports that he did not use the word *motivation*; he even avoided discussing how the probability of victimization differed across groups, "since that would bring up the forbidden topic of motivation" (Clarke and Felson, 1993, p. 2). Yet, Cohen and Felson did not rule out the use of motivation explanations; they felt that these "might in the future be applied to the analysis of offenders and their inclinations as well" (1979, p. 605).

Until recently, most empirical examinations of routine activities theory have been macro-level approaches, used mainly to explain the influence of lifestyle on crime. It is noted particularly that some locations (e.g., "hot spots") are more likely than others to become crime scenes (Roncek and Maier, 1991). For example, McCleary (2008) found that when Lion's Den "adult superstore" opened up on a highway off-ramp near a small rural village in the United States, total crime in that community increased by 60 percent. Two years later, the Lion's Den closed and total crime in the village dropped by roughly 60 percent.[3] Sometimes these factors are conflated: for example, the notion that because students tend to be victimized by students, female students proximity to campuses (hot spots) can be viewed as placing them into contact with likely offenders (Fisher, Daigle, and Cullen, 2010; Schwartz et al., 2001).

Prior to Stack et al.'s (2004) study, routine activities theory was never used in pornography research despite its overall popularity. Their application is as follows:

> [P]ersons with greater computer skills and with ownership of the relevant software might be more apt to take advantage of cyber porn opportunities than ones lacking in these resources. Further, the presence of children in the home may reduce opportunities for cyber pornography. Children can act as guardians and report the use of pornography to other adults in the home; children can also reduce opportunities for viewing porn on the family computer by increasing demand for limited Internet time. They may need to use the family's computer for school assignments, computer games, chat rooms, email, and other uses. In particular, the presence of teenage children may represent the greatest threat to discovery and the greatest competing demand for computer time for potential adult cyber porn offenders.

Stack et al. are commended for extending social scientific empirical and theoretical work on cyber pornography out of the realm of psychology, which, prior to their research, dominated the extant literature. Moreover, their study found direct relationships between some social bond variables (religious, marital, and political bonds) and cyber porn use. They also found some support for their rendition of opportunity theory. People with greater knowledge of Internet-oriented computer technology were more likely to use cyber porn.

What is unclear, though, is the type of pornography Stack et al.'s respondents consumed. For example, participants were "asked if they had visited a sexually explicit website during the last 30 days" (p. 80). Thus, it is impossible to discern the number of viewers who consumed child and/or adult porn. Furthermore, Stack et al. did not include measures of broader social and cultural forces, such as patriarchy. Such macro-level factors, according to feminist scholars, are key correlates of pornography consumption and it is to more gendered interpretations that we now turn.

FEMINIST THEORIES

Defining feminism is the subject of much debate. However, one thing leading experts in the field all agree with is that "feminism is not merely about adding women onto the agenda" (Currie and MacLean, 1993, p. 6). Here, consistent with many other progressive scholars, we offer Kathleen Daly and Meda Chesney-Lind's (1988) definition, which is still one of the most widely read and used offerings. Feminism refers to "a set of strategies about women's oppression and a set of strategies for change" (p. 502). For Corsianos (2009), "Feminism advocates social equality between 'women' and 'men' and opposes patriarchal ideologies, social systems, and structures" (p. 47). Still, not all feminists think alike and there are at least twelve variants of feminist theories of crime (Corsianos, 2009; Maidment, 2006; Renzetti, 2013).

Nonetheless all feminists prioritize gender, which is not the same as sex even though both terms are often incorrectly used interchangeably. Gender is the "socially defined expectations, characteristics, attributes, roles, responsibilities, activities, and practices that constitute masculinity, femininity, gender identity, and gender expressions" (Flavin and Artz, 2013, p. 11). Sex, on the other hand, refers to the biologically based categories of "female" and "male," which are stable across history and cultures (Dragiewicz, 2009). For instance, it is men who primarily commit violent crime, but many countries have markedly lower rates of violence than those of the United States, the Russian Federation, or Columbia (Currie, 2009, 2012). So, if "boys will be boys," they "will be so differently" (Kimmel, 2000), depending on where they live, their peer groups, social class position and race, and a host of other variables (DeKeseredy and Schwartz, 2010; Messerschmidt, 2014).

Most feminists also agree that nearly all societies are patriarchal (Renzetti, 2012; Corsianos, 2009). There are conflicting definitions of patriarchy and it is a heavily contested concept (Hunnicutt, 2009), but it is still common to draw from prominent violence against women scholars Dobash and Dobash (1979), who contend that patriarchy consists of two key elements: a structure and an ideology. Structurally, "patriarchy" is a hierarchical organization in which males have more power and privilege than women. As an ideology, patriarchy rationalizes itself. This means it provides a means of creating acceptance of subordination not only by those who benefit from such actions, but even by those who are placed in such subordinate positions by society (DeKeseredy and Schwartz, 2013; Corsianos, 2009). For Corsianos (2009), "Sexism is the ideological basis for patriarchy and is the belief that one sex is superior to the other" (p. 48).

Most definitions of patriarchy are simple, like the one above, but in reality there are different types of male power systems. *Societal patriarchy* is often used to refer to male domination at the societal level, but there is a subsystem often called *familial patriarchy*, that refers to male control in domestic or intimate settings (Barrett, 1985; Eisenstein, 1980; Ursel, 1986). However, even if patriarchy is divided into these two variants, neither can be understood without reference to each other (Smith, 1990). As Hunnicutt (2009) puts it, "Micro- and macro-patriarchal systems exist symbiotically. Interpersonal dynamics are nested within the macro-level gender order" (pp. 557–558).

Early Feminist Perspectives on Pornography

Patriarchy is of central concern to one widely cited type of feminist understanding of pornography: radical feminism. Arguably, of all the variants of feminist thought scattered through the literature, it is radical feminism that has had the greatest impact on the sociological study of pornography, as well as violence against women (DeKeseredy and Schwartz, 2011). Radical feminists contend that the most important set of social relations in any society is found in patriarchy and that throughout the world, females are the most oppressed social group, while regardless of their race/ethnicity and social class, men always have more power and privilege (Renzetti,

2012, 2013). For Radical feminists, women's oppression is the oldest form of oppression; it's widespread; it's international; and, it's the hardest to eradicate (Corsianos, 2009).

It must be emphasized at the outset that radical feminists are not against the depiction of sex, but rather how sex is featured in contemporary pornography, which as we frequently mentioned, is violent and racist. Pioneering radical feminist scholars, such as Catharine MacKinnon (1983, 1989), Susan Brownmiller (1975), Andrea Dworkin (1981), and Diana Russell (1990), made an argument that many feminists (e.g., Dines 2010; Jensen, 2007) still agree with today; that is, that common representations of "women" in mainstream porn today are violent; they eroticize male dominance and female submission; and, they reinforce and cause women's subordination (Bart, 1985). Radical feminists then and now also contend that pornography "lies about women's sexuality" (Lacombe, 1988, p. 41). Indeed, while we know that women featured in much of today's porn suffer from violent and degrading behaviors committed against them primarily by men, they are typically portrayed as enjoying the various degradation ceremonies they are put through during the filming process. As well, gonzo porn and other disturbing sexually explicit media send out a strong message that women's primary purpose is to satisfy men's desires.

While the above arguments are shared by most anti-porn feminists, there is no consensus about the development and implementation of policies that target porn, and conflicting feminist policy responses to porn have existed for decades. Still, the early work of radical feminists advanced how pornography is now perceived in academic and other circles. What Lacombe (1988) stated nearly 30 years ago still holds true today:

> Pornography is not seen, anymore, as the mere depiction of nudity, but more of a cultural form of dominance. By making a critique of the assumptions about female sexuality embodied in the sexual representations, anti-pornography feminists were able to demonstrate that pornography is a reflection of a fundamental antagonism between the sexes.
>
> (p. 41)

Notwithstanding Lacombe's praise for radical feminist interpretations of porn, radical feminism in general is accused of making several of what Messerschmidt (1993) refers to as some "theoretical errors." For example, not all men are oppressors, and there is a growing pro-feminist men's movement that confronts patriarchal practices, including the production and consumption of porn, on a daily basis (DeKeseredy and Schwartz, 2013; Funk, 2006; Katz, 2006; Renzetti, 2012). As well, radical feminism views gender as strictly dichotomous. For instance, all men are painted as corrupt and obsessed with death, while all women are seen as inherently nurturing and life-giving (Tong, 1989). This "black-and-white distinction" ignores the fact that there are various types of masculinities and femininities that are historically, socially, culturally, and psychologically constructed (Corsianos, 2012; Messerschmidt and Tomsen, 2012). Moreover, radical feminism tends to overlook that gender inequality intersects with other types of inequality, such as racism and social class inequality (Corsianos, 2009; Burgess-Proctor, 2006; Renzetti, 2013). More recent feminist theories address this concern and there is an emerging body of feminist knowledge coined as *intersectionality*. This school of thought, according to Crenshaw (2000), "addresses the manner in which racism, patriarchy, class oppression, and other discriminatory systems create background inequalities that structure the relative positions of women, races, ethnicities, classes, and the like" (p. 8). Intersectionality is front and center in an emerging body of critical criminological literature[4] on the lives of African-American girls and women. Two examples that immediately come to mind are the writings of Nikki Jones (2010) and Hillary Potter (2008).

We do not, however, want to give readers unfamiliar with the feminist pornography literature the impression that contemporary scholars informed by radical feminism, such as Dines (2010) and Jensen (2007), ignore race/ethnicity. On the contrary, this factor is an integral part of their analyses.

A Feminist/Male Peer Support Model of Pornography Consumption and Violence against Women

While the relationship between pornography and violence against women is highly complex (Jensen, 2007), a relatively new body of sociological knowledge strongly indicates that male peer support is a major part of the equation. Originally developed by Walter DeKeseredy (1988), this concept is defined as the attachments to male peers and the resources that these men provide that encourage and legitimate woman abuse. The pornography offerings crafted by DeKeseredy and Olsson (2011) and DeKeseredy and Schwartz (2013) begin by asserting that a substantial number of male actions, either individually or in peer groups, are micro-social expressions of broader patriarchal forces. Put another way, in the words of Maier and Bergen (2012), the foundation for male peer support for violence against women "rests on the normalization and acceptance of gender inequality and the recognition that 'real' men are superior to women and naturally have authority over them" (p. 332). This statement points to the influence of radical feminism on the theoretical work done by DeKeseredy and his two colleagues to be reviewed below.

A few studies found that the contribution of pornography to woman abuse in intimate heterosexual relationships is related to male peer support (DeKeseredy and Schwartz, 1998a, 2009; Schwartz and DeKeseredy, 1998). Further, some men learn to sexually objectify women through their exposure to pornographic media (Funk, 2006; Jensen, 1995). Consider what Kimmel (2008) found in his research on "guys" (men between the ages of 16 and 26): "Guys tend to like the extreme stuff, the double penetration and humiliating scenes; they watch it together, in groups of guys, and they make fun of the women in the scene." Additionally, Kimmel is correct to point out that, "Violence and aggression in pornography is more likely to be skewed toward the younger consumer" (p. 181).

It is also well documented empirically that many college men belong to "hypererotic subcultures" in which members have high expectations of having sex and then end up feeling disappointed or angry if women reject their advances (DeKeseredy and Schwartz, 2013; Kanin, 1985). In other words, these men are taught by their peers to *expect* to engage in a very high level of consensual intercourse, or what to them is sexual conquest. The problem, of course, is that for most men such goals are impossible to achieve. When they fall short of what they see as their friends' high expectations, and perhaps short of what they believe their friends are all actually achieving, some of these men experience *relative deprivation*. This sexual frustration, caused by a "reference-group-anchored sex drive" can result in predatory sexual conduct (Kanin, 1967a; Schwartz and DeKeseredy, 1997). The men are highly frustrated, not because they are deprived of sex in some objective sense, but because they feel inadequate or unable to engage in what they have defined as the proper amount of sex.

Hypererotic subcultures on college campuses have existed for decades, but they are now heavily influenced by a combination of the new "hook up culture"[5] and pornography (Freitas, 2013; Kimmel, 2008). According to Dines (2010):

> Given the increasing presence of hooking up in the culture, especially on college campuses, these men's perceptions that other guys seem to have no problem finding sex is not completely inaccurate. Where they seem to lose touch with reality is in the degree to which they assume this is the norm. In the porn world of never-ending sex, every interaction with a woman—be it a student, a doctor, a maid, a teacher, or just a stranger—ends up sexualized. Add to this the stories that men regale each other about their latest conquest, stories that often sound like the porn movie they just watched, and you have constructed a world of constant male access to every woman a man meets. When the real world doesn't play out like this, then disappointment and anger make sense.
>
> (p. 89)

Using pornographic videos to strengthen male "misogynist bonds" dates back to the 1890s (Slayden, 2010). Cinematic pornography originated in 16 mm silent films,

> usually shown in private all-male "smokers" in such contexts as bachelor parties and the like. Within such a context, the men laughed and joked and talked among themselves while watching the sexually explicit films about women, who though were absent from the audience, were the likely butt of the jokes, laughing, and rude remarks.
>
> (Lehman, 2006, p. 4)

Indeed, much has changed since then. Let's fast forward from the 1890s to the 2005 event described by Robert Jensen in Box 3.1. It is further support for the "normalization of pornography" thesis advanced by him, Gail Dines (2010), and a host of other feminists.

Although porn performers are not physically in their viewing areas, many college men behave similarly to the men featured in Box 3.1 while watching porn videos together. As Kimmel (2008) frequently discovered:

Box 3.1 LAS VEGAS ADULT ENTERTAINMENT EXPO

I am at the Adult Entertainment Expo in Las Vegas in January 2005. At one of the 300 exhibitor booths on the floor of the Sands Expo Center is Tiffany Holiday, a woman who performs in pornographic movies. She is kissing and touching another female performer, and a crowd of men gathers around. There are rules for how much actual sexual activity can take place on the convention floor, and the two women are pushing the boundary. The crowd encourages them to go further.

The other woman leaves, and Tiffany begins to stimulate masturbation, all the while talking dirty to the men gathered around her. The crowd swells to 50 men. I'm stuck in the middle, holding a microphone for a documentary film crew. Emboldened by the size of the crowd, the men's chants for more explicit sex grow louder and more boisterous. Holiday responds in kind, encouraging the men to tell her what they like. The exchange continues, intensifying to the point where the men are moving as a unit—like a mob.

Men's bodies are pressed against each other as each one vies for the best view of the woman's breasts, vagina, and anus. Many of the men are using cameras, camcorders, or cell phones to record the scene. It's difficult not to notice—not to feel—that the men pressed up against me have erections. It's difficult not to conclude that if there weren't security guards on the floor, these men would likely gang-rape Tiffany Holiday.

This is an expression of the dominant masculinity in the United States today. It is the masculinity of a mob, ready to rape.

Source: Jensen (2007, p. 1).

So what do the guys do? They get angry. Each time I happened on a group of guys engaged in group pornography consumption, they spent a good deal of time jiving with each other about what they'd like to do to the girl on the screen, yelling at her, calling her a whore and a bitch and cheering on the several men who will proceed to penetrate her simultaneously.

(p. 187)

Many, if not most, people assume that little crime occurs in rural communities, an assumption promoted by the media, lay conversations, and even criminological research, which mainly focuses on urban lawbreaking (Corsianos, 2015; 2012; Donnermeyer and DeKeseredy, 2014). According to newspaper reporter Theresa Boyle (2007), "After all, conventional wisdom holds that the big, bad city is the root of all evil. Small towns are supposed to be peaceful and serene" (p. A19). For numerous rural women, however, nothing can be further from the truth. There is much woman abuse in rural areas and recent studies show that it is fueled, in part, by male peer support and pornography (DeKeseredy et al., 2014).[6] For example, some rural Ohio survivors of separation/divorce sexual assault interviewed by

DeKeseredy and Schwartz (2009) told them that their partners consumed porn with their male friends while drinking excessive amounts of alcohol. One interviewee who experienced this problem described this episode:

> They were drinking and carrying on and they had, um, they had a bunch of porno stuff in the garage, and I had walked in and I had started to tear it up. And I was, I was, I thought it was gross. I was mad at it. I was mad at him for being around it. And he just started charging after me, and I started running to my car as fast as I could. And he got into the car and he threw me down in the seat and he just kept punching me, punching me.
>
> (p. 74)

Regardless of whether they consumed it in groups, 65 percent of the estranged partners of the 43 women in DeKeseredy and Schwartz's (2009) study viewed pornography, and 30 percent reported that porn was involved in sexually abusive events they experienced. Further, there is now evidence suggesting that rural boys consume pornography more than do their urban counterparts (Betowski, 2007; DeKeseredy et al., 2013). As well, the states with the most pornographic subscription rates in the United States (e.g., Mississippi) have large rural populations.

Male peer support theorists DeKeseredy and Olsson (2011) and DeKeseredy and Schwartz (2013) also point to the fact that some men abuse female intimates and consume pornography but do not view it or read it in groups gathered at one particular place. Moreover, they may not directly interact with abusive or sexist peers on a face-to-face basis. This is not to say, though, that they are not influenced to consume porn and/or victimize women by male peers. We are now seeing the rapid development of online communities with members who never come into face-to-face contact with each other but frequently exchange written, audio, and visual communication with their peers (Doring, 2009). Kimmel's online research (2008) summarized below provides further evidence of this subculture:

> [O]nline chat rooms are, by their nature, spaces of social interaction among men. These chat rooms are the closest thing to a pornographic locker room in which bonding is often accomplished by competing with the other guys. In the online chat rooms, a description of a violent sexual encounter might be followed by another user's "Oh yeah, well, last night I did this to the woman I was with . . ." which would be followed by another response designed to top even that. The competition can become heated—and violent—rather quickly. What we had stumbled on was the "homosocial" element in heterosexual porn viewing, the way in which anything, including intimacy with a member of the opposite sex, can be turned into a competitive moment with other guys.
>
> (p. 187)

It should be noted in passing that there is another type of online male peer support subculture, one that consists of anti-feminist fathers' rights (FR) activists. Based on her in-depth ethnographic analysis, Dragiewicz (2011) concludes:

The use of FR Web sites as places for like-minded men to seek out and receive peer support for violence-supportive attitudes is a serious concern for those interested in decreasing domestic violence, especially when we recognize their similarity to batterer accounts. The compatibility of FR commentary on VAWA with patriarchal peer support for violence should not go unnoticed.

(p. 137)

More recently, Kimmel (2013) found that, in their "man caves" or "politically incorrect locker rooms," members of patriarchal FR groups sometimes explicitly advocate violence against women. Below is one example. It is a tirade posted online by Paul Elam, editor of the *Men's News Daily* site:

There are women, and plenty of them, for which [sic] a solid ass kicking would be the least they deserve. The real question here is not whether these women deserve the business end of a right hook, they obviously do, and some of them deserve one hard enough to leave them in an unconscious, innocuous pile on the ground if it serves to protect the innocent from imminent harm. The real question is whether men deserve to be able to physically defend themselves from assault . . . from a woman.

(cited in Kimmel, 2013, p. 118)[7]

Note, too, as exemplified in Box 3.2, that new cyberspace technology enables men to engage in the online victimization of women, such as what recently happened to Stoney Creek, Ontario resident, Vanessa Bruno. This involves men "virtually assaulting," "virtually raping," or "cyber stalking" women who use the Internet (Kendall, 2003; Tucker, Fraser, and Shulruff, 2008). There are also "porn horror" sites, rape sites, and video games such as Rapelay (Jones, 2010), in which players direct a man to rape a mother and her two young daughters at an underground station before raping a selection of other females (Kome, 2009).

Although rarely studied, online communities that seek out porn that combines sex with violence are "part of a broader subculture of sexual deviance that legitimizes various forms of deviant sexuality" (Stack et al., 2004). Also, in recent times, there have been a number of highly publicized cases involving men posting their brutal group behaviors on social media. One recent example is the case of a rape in Steubenville, a small city of about 18,000 in a predominantly rural county located in the eastern, Appalachian region of Ohio. The events of Steubenville should give us pause to consider the seriousness of media's impact in real-life terms, for in this town, two football players were convicted of raping a local girl of high school age while she was drunk after attending several parties held on August 11, 2012, right before the new school year began. What brought this incident to light were the posts, videos, and photographs on YouTube, Instagram, and Facebook of the incident by those who were there (New York Times, 2012). It was news and "grist for the rumor mill" throughout the area the next day. But this example is not just about those who callously posted their acts of gendered violence on social media outlets, others at the party who did nothing to stop the abuse, the pedestal on which football

---

Box 3.2 RAPE THREATS PART OF ONLINE HARASSMENT CASE AGAINST STONEY CREEK MAN

For 6 months, Vanessa Bruno was tormented by an anonymous online stalker. She says he figured out where she lived, threatened to wait outside her workplace to rape her and messaged her through a fake online account in the name of her brother, who recently committed suicide.

"I thought you were a strong, independent Italian woman! Hahahahaha you're nothing but another soon-to-be rape statistic," the stalker wrote on her blog. "Watch out b——, I'm gonna have you soon."

Bruno says the alleged perpetrator was a complete stranger to her.

The case comes at a time when much attention is being drawn to the gendered harassment women face online—in Toronto, where Gregory Alan Elliott, 53, is on trial after pleading not guilty to criminal harassment charges stemming from Twitter exchanges with women; and worldwide, most recently through a widely read and well-reviewed essay by American writer Amanda Hess for the *Pacific Standard*, "Why Women Aren't Welcome on the Internet."

Source: Dempsey (2014, pp. 1–2).

---

is placed in this city, or the tight-knit relationships between the sheriff and other community leaders with the football coach, team, and parents of the players. It is also about the reaction of several young college aged men, one of who was enrolled at The Ohio State University and from the same county where the incident occurred. Caught on a cell phone camera video by a friend while he was drunk at a party, he laughingly proclaimed, "they raped her harder than that cop raped Marsellus Wallace in *Pulp Fiction*. Have you seen that?" He then proceeded to concoct several other disturbing analogies, making fun of the incident as if it was the replay of a football game telecast. Referring to this young man's insensitive quips as a form of comedy, another party goer tosses out the compliment "He comes up with them so fast." That video also went viral, adding another layer of shame to the Steubenville case, and to The Ohio State University, even though the student has not re-enrolled there (The Atlantic Wire, 2013).

Since the late 1990s Walter DeKeseredy and Martin Schwartz (1998b) have continually argued that the sharing of cyber porn helps create and maintain patriarchal male peer groups. This sharing reinforces attitudes that reproduce and reconstitute ideologies of male dominance by approvingly depicting women as objects to be conquered and consumed (DeKeseredy and Schwartz, 2013). Such sharing also makes it difficult for users to separate sexual fantasy from reality and assists them in their attempts to initiate female victims and break down their resistance to sexual acts (Dines, 2010).

The male peer support perspective, while informed by some qualitative and quantitative studies, has yet to actually be tested using original data. Hopefully, this issue will be addressed in the near future. Yet, given that DeKeseredy and Schwartz's previous male peer support theories garnered considerable empirical support,[8] we hypothesize that the offerings crafted by them and by DeKeseredy and Olsson will be empirically verified. Still, their work leaves some important questions unanswered. For example, where are we most likely to find cyber porn subcultures? Are white men more or less likely than African-American, Aboriginal, or Hispanic males to join and be influenced by pro-abuse male subcultures that distribute and consume cyber porn? These are important empirical questions that can only be answered empirically. Social scientific research on cyber porn is still in a state of infancy and much more research and theoretical work on a myriad of issues related to this social problem needs to be done.

SUMMARY

Statistics presented throughout this book show that a large number of men consume pornography and that the results of doing so can be deeply hurtful. Nonetheless, these data reflect only the tip of the iceberg: that which is reported to researchers. The next step for investigators is to develop new and innovative methods of gathering data on pornography use that minimize underreporting. Even so, to advance a better understanding of pornography use and its effects, and to both prevent and control the consumption of degrading and violent sexual media, more than just accurate data are required. We need to explain why people watch or read violent and abusive porn.

Unfortunately, theoretical developments have not kept pace with the burgeoning empirical literature on pornography and its effects. In this chapter, we reviewed the most well-known sociological accounts developed so far, but there is still much more theoretical work to do. Obviously, there are other factors that contribute to porn use and its negative outcomes. Nonetheless, the growing body of research on porn reveals that, like criminal conduct in general, pornography use and distribution is "predominantly social behavior" among younger men (Warr, 2002). Most such users are embedded in a network of friends with similar tastes, which is one of the key reasons why sociological theories are unquestionably necessary. Related to this point is the fact that we are surrounded by pornographic media and those who use it (Corsianos, 2007). A rich understanding of the topics covered in this book, then, necessitates that we travel down the social scientific path created for us by the late C. Wright Mills (1959) and continue to use the sociological imagination. Mills compels us to look beyond the personal troubles of one or two women assaulted by a male partner and rather to look at the broader problem of woman abuse in our society.

DISCUSSION QUESTIONS

1. What are the limitations to relying on individualistic explanations for consumption of violent porn?

2. How do feminist theories help us better understand men's consumption of hurtful porn?
3. What role does male peer support play in the mainstreaming of violence against women in sexual media?

NOTES

1. This section includes modified sections of work published previously by DeKeseredy and Olsson (2011) and DeKeseredy and Schwartz (1996, 2013).

2. This section includes revised sections of work published previously by Alvi, DeKeseredy, and Ellis (2000), DeKeseredy (2011b), DeKeseredy et al. (2013), DeKeseredy and Olsson (2011), DeKeseredy and Schwartz (1996, 2013), and Schwartz, DeKeseredy, Tait, and Alvi (2001).

3. Rural U.S. communities have become "pornified" due in large part to the Lion's Den chain (Donnermeyer and DeKeseredy, 2014; Paul, 2005). In fact, at least a third of their stores are located off a U.S. interstate highway and in or near towns of 16,000 or fewer residents (DeKeseredy et al., 2013; Howlett, 2012). Also referred to as "freeway porn stores," Kat Sunlove, an adult movie actress turned lobbyist working for the Free Speech Center views these stores and the pornification of rural highways as "capitalism at its best . . . This is a transformed industry, and businesses are just following the market" (cited in Howlett, 2012, p. 1).

4. Critical criminologists view hierarchical social stratification and inequality along class, racial/ethnic, and gender lines as the major sources of crime. See DeKeseredy and Dragiewicz (2012, 2014) for information on the history of critical criminology and contemporary critical criminologists' major empirical, theoretical, and political contributions.

5. "Hooking up" is an ambiguous term and it means different things to different people. Generally, the phrase refers to a casual sexual encounter (with no promise of commitment) ranging from kissing to sexual intercourse (Bogle, 2008).

6. There is growing evidence that rural U.S. women are at much greater risk of experiencing intimate violence than are women living in other parts of the country. For instance, using 1992–2009 National Crime Victimization Survey (NCVS) data, Rennison, DeKeseredy, and Dragiewicz (2012) found that exiting relationships are significantly more dangerous for rural women than for their urban and suburban counterparts, Rural separated women experience intimate rape/sexual assault at rates more than three times higher than their urban counterparts. Rural separated women, too, are raped/sexually assaulted by an intimate partner at rates about 1.6 times higher than similarly situated suburban women. Using the same data set and combining different types of violence into one dependent variable, Rennison, DeKeseredy, and Dragiewicz (2013) also found that rural divorced and separated females are intimately victimized at rates exceeding separated/divorced urban women. Plus, they uncovered that rural females have a higher rate of all kinds of intimate violence than do urban and suburban females.

7. Kimmel accessed this violent statement at www.avoiceformen.com/feminism/government-tyranny/when-is-it-ok-to-punch-your-wife-htm.

8. See DeKeseredy and Schwartz (2013) for a detailed review of all of their male peer support theories and the extensive array of quantitative and qualitative studies guided by them.

Chapter 4

Pornography and Violence against Women

> He would bring pornographic magazines, books, and paraphernalia into the
> bedroom with him and tell her that if she did not perform the sexual acts that
> were being done in the dirty books and magazines he would beat and kill her.
>
> (Jensen, 1998, p. 115)

THERE is an unsettling truth that even many feminist anti-violence activists and
practitioners rarely discuss—pornography plays a key role in women's experiences
of male violence in private places. As well, among the large, international group of
woman abuse scholars, very few of them research and theorize the connection
between porn and intimate violence. In the words of Shope (2004), "The paucity
of research on the effects of pornography on battered women is disturbing in light of
the research findings linking pornography to sexually aggressive behavior, particularly among angered men" (p. 66). However, things are slowly changing in the
social scientific community. Recall from reading Chapter 3 that a growing number
of academics, such as the authors of this book, treat pornography and its negative
effects as both major social problems and subjects worthy of in-depth scholarly
inquiry. The main objective of this chapter is to review the current state of empirical
knowledge on the association between hurtful pornography and men's violent
victimization of current and former intimate female partners. Men's abuse of other
women in other ways, including pornographic cyber-bulling, will also be covered,
as well as violence against women in the porn industry.

THE CAUSAL CONNECTION DEBATE[1]

Since the late 1970s, North American researchers have generated extensive data
on the extent, distribution, correlates, sources, and consequences of woman abuse
in heterosexual relationships. During the same stretch of time, research into erotica
and pornography, and their potential effects on men's behavior also expanded. The

bulk of the early studies employed experimental designs in laboratory settings and several projects found that exposure to more graphic and violent images changed people's attitudes toward women and rape (e.g., Briere and Malamuth, 1983; Linz, 1989). Interestingly, few studies took on the problem of the potential for rebound effects. Simply put, men enter the experimental labs with relatively good attitudes toward women. They watch a sexually graphic and violent video, and then are shown to have more troublesome attitudes toward women. The problem is that this is not the first time these men have ever been exposed to pornographic media. For example, Garcia (1986) found that the overwhelming majority of undergraduate men have read pornographic books and seen pornographic movies that include forced sex and sex with violence, with 95.7 percent having seen movies featuring sexual intercourse, 83.5 percent oral sex, and 68.7 percent forced sex. Within one previous year alone, another group of undergraduate males reported that 81 percent had used pornography, with 41 percent and 35 percent using violent and sexually violent porn, respectively (Demare, Briere, and Lipps, 1988). So, if exposure to such media lowers one's opinions of women and legitimizes or at least desensitizes one to rape, how is it that researchers continued to find subjects who begin the study with high scores on tests measuring attitudes toward women, and a high sensitivity toward rape (Schwartz, 1987)? Wouldn't their previous exposure to this media have affected them enough to lower their pre-test scores dramatically?

One possible explanation for the problem is that there is some sort of rebound effect, where the worsened attitude toward women is short-lived. Unfortunately, until the late 1990s, there was little information on the extent to which graphic sexual imagery affects men's aggressive or violent behavior outside the lab setting. Again, most of the evidence produced prior to the late 1990s came from "artificial" lab studies leading critics to claim that there is little to support any links with "real world" behavior (Berger, Searles, and Cottle, 1991; Brannigan and Goldenberg, 1987). Indeed, many of the lab scientists who conducted the best known studies said that politicians went too far in suggesting that experimental lab findings are equivalent to the same effects taking place in society (Segal, 1993). Certainly, there were some attempts at imaginative alternative methodology. Jensen (1995, 1996), for example, used personal histories and narrative accounts of men who used porn. In another early attempt to look at "real world" effects, Demare, Lips, and Briere (1993) tied the use of sexually violent pornography to a self-reported likelihood of committing rape or using sexual force. Still, this only measures a self-reported proclivity, which may or may not be related to actual behavior.

The lack of information on the relationship between reading porn and acting aggressively is worth noting, as it was one of the earliest inquiries in this field. It was the primary question that motivated both the U.S. official panels set up to investigate the issue: the President's Commission on Pornography and Obscenity (1970) and the Attorney General's Commission on Pornography (1986). These two commissions were at opposite ends of the scientific and political spectrum: the earlier group denied a causal relationship, while the latter group found one. Ultimately, the 1986 report skillfully grafted a feminist anti-pornography argument onto a conservative political agenda (Schwartz and DeKeseredy, 1998; Vance, 1993), so that the commission was able to argue that proof of direct harm was not necessary. Rather, simply showing that a population that does not view and approve of pornography would be sufficient to sustain an argument that pornography is harmful. Interestingly, the Canadian Supreme Court, after putting together an internal study commission that rejected these arguments, proceeded in R. vs. Butler (1992, S.C.J. No. 15) to accept this exact position, in which has come to be called the "harm" argument (Einsiedel, 1995).

For sure, as Russell (1995) contends, it would be foolish to argue that there is some sort of automatic connection between graphic sex and woman abuse. Some unknown but presumably large numbers of violent pornography consumers do not rape women. Moreover, some women enjoy or become sexually aroused by different types of pornography, and some women enjoy acting out behaviors learned from sexually graphic media. However, what more contemporary researchers are finding in this online age is that there is another group of women who report that pornography is related to their current and/or former male partner's abusive behaviors. More will be said about these women and the men who abuse them shortly. Nevertheless, it is first necessary to emphasize that despite the emergence of research outside lab settings, it is still unclear whether pornography of any sort directly causes woman abuse. A long-term and expensive longitudinal design is required to determine if such as relationship exists (DeKeseredy and Schwartz, 2013). Additionally, there are some important competing arguments. For instance, for men who physically, sexually, and psychologically abuse women, pornography may well be just one more weapon in their arsenal. Thus, a man who cares that his partner would be scared or angry might not expose her to the lessons he learned from a pornographic video, while his abusive friend might try to force his intimate female partner to act out such scenes over her objections (DeKeseredy and Schwartz, 2009).

In a somewhat related argument, the same factors that cause a man to abuse women may well also cause him to watch Internet porn. Put another way, the woman abuse came first, followed by the interest in pornography. In these scenarios, eliminating pornography might not have an effect on the amount of woman abuse, since the men are generally abusive anyway (DeKeseredy and Schwartz, 1998a).

Finally, there is the argument that the problem is not the sexually graphic images at all, but the images of violence (Schwartz, 1987). In this scenario, exposure to all forms of violent behavior can be considered dangerous. In the field of graphic images, this argument would not dilute our assertion, which is that mutually respectful sexual imagery is not a problem. Rather, it is the introduction and integration of violent imagery with sexually graphic scenes that is the problem.

While we might not yet understand the specific dynamics of how it operates, there is ample empirical evidence showing that violent pornography is a component of woman abuse and that many abusive men are graduates of what Lundy Bancroft (2002) refers to as "the Pornography School of Sexuality" (p. 231). Maybe, then, it would be best to follow Robert Jensen's (2007) advice: "Rather than discussing simple causation, we should consider how various factors, in feminist philosopher

Marilyn Frye's terms 'make something inviting.' In those terms, pornography does not cause rape, rather helps make rape inviting" (p. 103).

In their commentary on the current state of research on pornography and violence against women, DeKeseredy and Schwartz (2013) address another gap in the literature. They note that it is still unclear where the majority of viewers of pornography obtain or access these images, and whether some forms of access facilitate male-to-female physical and sexual violence more than other types of access. In other words, are men who view, listen to, or read pornography and who abuse women more likely to seek sexually explicit material online or elsewhere? What Ferguson (1996) stated 17 years ago is still relevant: "Pornography (both criminal and non-criminal) does exist in Cyberspace, and can be accessed and downloaded by virtually anyone with the appropriate knowledge regarding how to go about obtaining it" (p. 27). One certainty is that children and youth today are much more sophisticated than any earlier generation in accessing computer sites, including those with barriers to entry by youth. Still, until conclusive evidence is generated and corroborated, it is wrong to conclude that male pornography users who abuse women primarily consume Internet porn. Nonetheless, as Dines and Jensen (2008) observe:

> While there are few studies of the effects of Internet pornography, past research suggests that this increase in pornography consumption is implicated in greater levels of male physical and sexual violence against women and children.
>
> (p. 366)

BEYOND THE LABORATORY: THE EARLY STUDIES[2]

Diana Russell made numerous important contributions to a social scientific understanding of woman abuse, including its relationship to pornography. She is, to the best of our knowledge, the first scholar to develop a large-scale, representative sample survey of violence against women that included this question (see Russell, 1982, 1990): "Have you ever been upset by anyone trying to get you to do what they'd seen in pornographic pictures, movies, or books?" It is essential to note that this question does not cover situations where the woman was not offended by the actions of the porn user, or where she welcomed suggestions. As Russell (1995) states, "Imitating pornography is only cause for concern if the behavior imitated is violent or abusive, or if the behavior is not wanted by the recipient" (p. 65). It may be that more people engage in this imitation than are made upset by it. Bryant (1985) found that about one quarter of the men he questioned said they did "actually experiment or try any of the behaviors depicted" within a few days of being exposed to X-rated materials. This is a higher percentage than is usually found of women who report being offended by such requests.

Still, many women are upset by these demands. Several studies used Russell's question to ask women about their experiences and the data support this observation.

Based on data gleaned from 930 women in San Francisco, Russell (1990) found that 10 percent of the adult women in her sample answered "yes" to this question. Similarly, using data generated by the late Michael D. Smith's (1987) Toronto woman abuse study, Harmon and Check (1989) found that about 9 percent of the female respondents gave an affirmative answer in this telephone survey, while 24 percent of Senn's (1993) sample of 96 University of Calgary students said that they had experienced this.

Researchers commonly have the problem of determining whether or not to replicate previous studies. On the one hand, using a variation of the same question that other researchers have used allows for a comparison of current data to previously gathered data. On the other hand, there is value to proposing new questions. In their Canadian national survey (CNS) of woman abuse in university/college dating, DeKeseredy and Schwartz (1998a) chose the first path and used a slightly modified version of Russell's (1990) question. In this study, female respondents were asked to answer yes or no:

> Thinking about your entire university and/or college career, have you ever been upset by dating partners and/or boyfriends trying to get you to do what they had seen in pornographic media?

Men were asked a similar question: whether they had ever "upset dating partners and/or girlfriends by trying to get them to do what you had seen in pornographic pictures, movies, or books."

Of the 1,638 women in DeKeseredy and Schwartz's sample who had both dated and answered the question on pornography, 137 (8.4 percent) stated that they were upset by their dating partners trying to get them to do what they had seen in pornographic media. This is very similar to the 10 percent figure that Russell (1990) reports for her similar question, although it should be noted that, for the most part, Russell interviewed women significantly older than those who participated in DeKeseredy and Schwartz's study. Consider, too, that 6.8 percent of the 1,307 men in the sample admitted that they had upset their dating partners by trying to get them to imitate porn.

In some studies, women who had suffered other types of victimization were also likely to report that they experienced this behavior as abusive. Russell (1990), for example found that for the women in her sample who were married and had been raped by their husband, the percent that answered the above question in her survey rose to 24 percent. Harmon and Check (1989) discovered that women who had been physically abused were three times more likely to be have been upset by being asked to imitate pornography (10.4 percent) than women who had not been physically abused (3.6 percent). What was most important to DeKeseredy and Schwartz's (1998a) research was that they found a significant relationship between being upset by men's attempts to imitate pornographic scenes and sexual victimization. Of those who were sexually abused, 22.3 percent had also been upset by attempts to get them to imitate pornographic scenarios. Only 5.8 percent of the women who were not victimized reported being upset by pornography. These figures compare well with Itzin and Sweet's (1992) report of the British Cosmopolitan Survey, although their crude methodology and cruder style of reporting the results make any real comparison impossible.

Again, 6.8 percent of the men in DeKeseredy and Schwartz's study reported that they upset their dating partners by getting them to imitate pornography. As well, the men were more likely to admit being forcible sexual victimizers if they also admitted to upsetting a woman this way. Almost four times as many upsetters (9.3 percent) as nonupsetters (2.4 percent) also admitted to committing a forcible sexual victimization after high school.

The relationship for sexual violence also holds for physical violence. Like some of the survivors of wife rape included in Bergen's (1996) sample, CNS female participants who indicated that they were physically assaulted once since leaving high school were also much more likely to have been upset by being asked to do what their dating partners had seen in pornographic pictures, movies, and so on. Consider the vicious behavior described below by one of the wife rape survivors interviewed by Bergen (1996):

> He was really into watching porno movies, and he tried to make me do all sorts of things. And I [didn't] like it. He hurt my stomach so bad because I was pregnant, and he was making me do these things. I think he's a sadist—he pulls my hair and punches me and slaps me and makes me pass out.
>
> (p. 18)

Of the female CNS respondents who reported being physically abused in a dating relationship, 15.4 percent also reported being upset by pornography. Only 4.5 percent of those who were not physically victimized reported being upset. Turning to the men, one third of all those who admitted to upsetting a woman with requests to imitate pornography also admitted to physically abusing a woman after high school. Of those who did not admit to upsetting a woman, 17.2 percent admitted to physical abuse. Although it is not uncommon to point to fraternity houses as a source of pornography influences (e.g., DeKeseredy and Olsson, 2011; Kimmel, 2008; Sanday, 1990), CNS data show that there was no difference between fraternity members and other men in the rates at which they admit to upsetting a woman by trying to get her to imitate pornography.

Moving outside the realm of college, Bergen (1996) asked a somewhat different question than Russell's (1990), but found that about one third of the marital rape survivors in her sample had husbands who viewed pornography and forced them to act out what they had seen. Sommers and Check (1987) found that women who were in battered women shelters were much more likely to report being made upset in this manner than mature undergraduates were. As well, though different questions were used, Cramer and McFarlane (1994) uncovered support for the finding that battered women have a special problem. In studying battered women who were filing criminal charges against their husbands, they found that 40 percent of husbands used pornography, and that the use of these materials was significantly associated with the participants being asked or forced to participate in violent acts.

These studies are commended for extending porn research beyond the problematic realm of the lab, and they produced important data for the time period in which they were conducted. Yet, an important difficulty in all empirical work of this kind is that the researcher has no control over the nature of the graphic material, or the definition being applied by the respondent. There is no way that the researcher can apply a single definition to pornography, or to control in any way an individual woman or man's definition of pornography. This is an ongoing problem in pornography research: pornography is commonly conflated into one type, and at the time the above studies were conducted, there was very little written on what McClintock (1993) calls "porn's kaleidoscopic variorum" (p. 115), or what Burstyn (1987) refers to as the "large and various discourse we call, all inclusively pornography" (p. 163). Today, however, there are scholarly books and articles that examine variations in erotica and pornography.[3]

Around the time when the studies reviewed in this section were done, there were basically two definitions of porn. "Conservative-moralist" researchers and theorists included in their definition of pornography any sexually explicit imagery, including people posing alone or couples engaging in consensual heterosexual behavior (Linz and Malamuth, 1991). On the other hand, anti-pornography feminists, such as Andrea Dworkin and Catherine MacKinnon, defined pornography as the graphic sexually explicit subordination of women through pictures or words (Schwartz, 1987). One solution was to specifically tell respondents to separate out and answer the question separately for mass-market magazines such as *Playboy*, and for more sexually graphic, or more violent media. Generally, studies that did this found that although there may be an effect from exposure to mass-market sexual themes (Linz and Malamuth, 1993), the reactions have not been the same as for exposure to graphic or sexually violent themes (Boeringer 1994; Garcia, 1986).

Thus, when asking women what makes them particularly upset, it is not likely that being asked to strike a pose like a centerfold in *Playboy* would elicit the most complaints. Generally, women are able to differentiate between violent and degrading imagery and imagery that is sexually graphic but neither violent nor degrading. For example, Senn (1993) found that the women in her sample rated erotic slides positively, nonviolent sexist and dehumanizing pornography slightly negatively, and violent sexist and dehumanizing porn very negatively. Cowan and Dunn (1994) similarly found that both men and women could and did make such distinctions.

Even so, in the research that used some variant of Russell's question, each female respondent was asked about whether men influenced by the entire universe of pornographic pictures, movies, or books have upset her by asking her to do what they had seen. Men were asked a similar question. As suggested, this lack of specificity places the researcher at the mercy of the definitions used by the respondent. Nonetheless, studies such as those done by Bergen (1996), DeKeseredy and Schwartz, Harmon and Check (1989), and Russell (1990) were among the first "real world" projects to reveal that pornography is related to sexual and physical violence.

CONTEMPORARY RESEARCH

The Internet was nowhere near an integral part of people's lives as it is now when the research reviewed in the previous section was conducted. Furthermore, pornography did not have the extraordinarily high rates of aggression and violence that exist today (Bridges and Anton, 2013). Conversely, there is no way of knowing whether the men who watch today's porn are at greater risk of abusing current or former female intimate partners than men who consumed violent sexual materials prior to the advent of the Internet. Nonetheless, what we do know today is what was confirmed in previous research: "[W]e certainly have enough evidence to warrant identifying pornography as a risk factor . . . associated with sexual violence among some populations" (Shope, 2004, p. 68). We also have enough evidence linking other forms of woman abuse to men's use of porn.

Youth and Violence against Women[4]

Nearly 15 years ago, Bergen and Bogle (2000) referred to pornography as a "training manual for abuse" (p. 231). Evidently, the preparation starts at a young age because boys see their first pornography site on average at 11 years of age (DeKeseredy, 2015; Dines 2010), and an unknown but large number go on to become woman abusers. Romito and Beltramini (2011) are correct to state, "Childhood and adolescence are key periods in relation to pornography exposure" (p. 1). In fact, adolescents are especially affected by perceived realism of porn because they often lack "real life" sexual experiences with women in which they can contextualize pornographic images of sex (Bridges and Anton, 2013; Peter and Valkenburg, 2010). Consider that one study found that exposure to pornography prior to the age of 10 was associated with increased risk of juvenile sexual perpetration in adjudicated boys (Hunter, Figueredo, and Malamuth, 2010). Keep in mind, too, that Leibowitz and Howard (2010) discovered that porn consumption was greater among adolescent boys convicted of sexual offenses compared to boys convicted of non-sexual crimes.

The correlation between pornography and youth violence against women is not restricted to North America. In Italy, one study of high school students uncovered strong associations between sexually harassing or raping peers and pornography consumption (Bonino, Ciairano, Rabaglietti, and Cattelino, 2006). Another Italian survey of high school students found that females exposed to psychological violence committed by family members and to sexual violence by any type of perpetrator were significantly more likely to watch pornography, especially violent porn, than females who were not exposed to such abuse (Romito and Beltramini, 2011). In Sweden, a study of 1,933 boys uncovered a higher rate of violent pornography use among those who reported sexually coercing someone compared to non-delinquent youth (Kjellgren, Priebe, Svedin, and Langstrom, 2010).

In sum, there is international evidence to support Bridges and Anton's (2013) claim that "exposure to pornography is particularly problematic for youth because they often lack healthy sexual relationships that counterbalance the degrading and depersonalizing images of sex often depicted in pornography" (p. 194). Arguably, that there is a relationship between porn consumption and youth violence against women in many parts of the world is also partly a function of the fact that male peer support for violence against women is an international phenomenon. Recall, the relationship between the male peer support, porn use, and woman abuse described in Chapter 3. International data reviewed by male peer support theorists DeKeseredy and Schwartz (2013) support what Lee Bowker (1983) said close to 30 years ago about all-male subcultures of violence:

> This is not a subculture that is confined to a single class, religion, occupational grouping or race. It is spread throughout all parts of society. Men are socialized by other subculture members to accept common definitions of the situation, norms, values, and beliefs about male dominance and the necessity of keeping their wives in line. These violence-supporting social relations may occur at any time and in any place.
>
> (pp. 135–136)

Male peer pressure that legitimates the sexual objectification of women and the sexual and/or physical abuse of them is found among African-American men in Chicago (Wilson, 1996), among Puerto Rican drug dealers in East Harlem, and poor African-American boys in parts of St. Louis (Bourgois, 1985; Miller, 2008), on Canadian college campuses and their immediate surroundings (DeKeseredy and Schwartz, 1998a), in rural Ohio and Kentucky (DeKeseredy and Donnermeyer, 2014; DeKeseredy and Schwartz, 2009; Websdale, 1998), and in rural New Zealand and rural South Africa (Campbell, 2000; Jewkes et al., 2006). There is also, as discussed in Chapter 3, evidence of the emergence of pro-abuse male peer groups in cyberspace, and many men who abuse women consume electronic pornography with their male friends.

Kimmel (2008), among others, correctly points out that most porn research is done by college professors who collect their data from male students in lab settings. We have already described the key problems with such research, but there is one more that Kimmel identifies that warrants attention: college researchers tend to "generalize their findings to 'men' in general, as if there were no differences among different age groups" (p. 180). While it is true, as noted in Chapter 3, that violent porn is skewed toward younger men, many older men consume pornography and the contexts and outcomes are often distinct from what Kimmel describes below:

> Adult men watch by themselves, or sometimes with a partner, and they tend to like the ones where the women look like they are filled with desire and experience pleasure. This is a significant counterpoint to those who feel called to mind the public's morality: It turns out pornography use over time does not up the ante and lead men toward increasingly violent and extreme images. Quite the opposite.
>
> (p. 181)

Kimmel does not offer any empirical evidence for this claim. Furthermore, there is sound research on violent porn and sexual arousal that strongly refutes his assertion. Note Bridges and Anton's (2013) brief summary of research on how porn affects the brain:

> Repeated exposure to pornographic images leads to desensitization to these images; therefore new, more arousing, and more intense pornographic images must be obtained to achieve the same degree of sexual excitation (Bridges, 2010). Over time, materials that are novel are necessarily going to contain more extreme sex acts (such as double penetrations), more paraphilic content (such as urinating on someone), and/or more extreme aggression and even violence— whatever it takes to give the viewer a "jolt" in short, even well-intentioned pornography users *may* find, with high frequency of use and continued repeated exposure, that they increasingly seek out the more problematic depictions of sex, those that are pornographic, violent, and degrading, compared with the more egalitarian, erotic depictions of sex that do not have negative effects on viewers.
>
> (p. 199)

As well, there is a small but emerging literature showing that adult men's porn consumption is related to violence against their current and former female partners. It is to this body of knowledge that we know turn.

Pornography and Violence in Adult Intimate Relationships[5]

The year 2000 marked a resurgence of "real world" research on this topic, starting with the work done by Bergen and Bogle (2000). The study involved rape crisis center staff completing 100 questionnaires based on phone and face-to-face interviews with sexual and physical assault survivors. Twenty-eight percent of the participants stated their abusers used pornography, but 58 percent stated that they didn't know if their assailants consumed it. Bergen and Bogle do point out, though, that since pornography is often viewed or read in private, it is quite likely that many members of this group of women were unaware of their partners' use of porn. Also, they state that women, who were assaulted by men they were not intimately involved with, such as strangers, co-workers, dates, and so on, were less likely to know if these perpetrators used porn unless it was mentioned or used during assaults.

Of the women who reported their partners' use of porn, 40 percent said that it was part of their abusive experiences. It is unclear from reading this study whether or not the perpetrators consumed Internet porn, but the types of porn used varied and many men used multiple types. The most common were magazines (54 percent) and videos (50 percent), and 18 percent of perpetrators used "home sex movies." As well, 13 percent of the total sample stated that they believed the assailants' porn use affected the type of abuse they went through. When, though, the analysis was restricted to women whose abusers used porn, 43 percent believed that it affected the type of abuse. Bergen and Bogle also found that 5 percent of the entire sample said that they were forced to pose for pornographic pictures and 12 percent stated that porn was imitated during their abusive experiences.

Two subsequent studies collected data from somewhat similar samples of women. For example, Shope (2004) analyzed data gathered from 1998 to 1991 by a New York battered women's program. The data were gleaned from 271 women, most of whom sought shelter from abusive men. Of the women whose abusers consumed porn, 58 percent stated that it affected their victimization. Moreover, as stated in Chapter 1, Shope found that abusers' use of porn nearly doubled the risk of a battered women being sexually assaulted. Keep in mind, as noted in her study, many women are pressured or forced to have sex with their abusers after being physically assaulted.

Simmons, Lehmann, and Collier-Tennison (2008) also analyzed data collected over a four-year period from abused women seeking social support. Interviews were conducted with 2,135 participants who were seen at a domestic violence shelter and the researchers uncovered an association between perpetrators' use of the sex industry (this included porn use) and women's victimization. Further, abusers' controlling behaviors were correlated with use of the sex industry, but Simmons et al. did not isolate the specific outcomes of perpetrators' consumption on these factors.

DeKeseredy and colleagues' (see DeKeseredy and Joseph, 2006; DeKeseredy and Schwartz, 2009; DeKeseredy, Schwartz, Fagen, and Hall, 2006) study of separation/divorce sexual assault in rural southeast Ohio is, to the best of our knowledge, the most recent "real world" study of the relationship between porn and rural woman abuse to be done at the time of writing this book. Face-to-face interviews with forty three women who were abused while they either wanted to end, were trying to end, or who have ended a relationship with a husband or live-in partner were conducted. As described in Chapter 3, 65 percent of these women's estranged partners viewed pornography and 30 percent of the sample stated that porn was involved in their sexual abuse. One man did the following to a respondent after discovering that she was on the verge of exiting the relationship:

> I walked into him masturbating in front of my children to *Penthouse*. . . . There were naked pictures, well not naked, but pictures of men in a bra and underwear that he had stolen and had developed.

DeKeseredy and his colleagues were told many other alarming stories about pornography, including those involving men using it to get their ex-partners to have sex with them again. One woman stated:

> Like he would, I would come to the house. Like he would call me and tell me that he wants to talk with me, and I would go to the house, and he would have a porn movie on, you know on television, when we're supposed to be talking about us. I sit down, and there's the porn movie, and then, he comes over, sits on top of me, and the whole nine yards starts.

Another woman said:

He acts like he's a porn star, you know what I mean. So there were times when he would pound, and when I use the word pound, that's lightly. And he would just pound until I would bleed and hurt for days. And he would just make me keep doing it every night. "You're my girlfriend. You want me to go somewhere else? Why won't you have sex with me?" Well, you know, and not even comfortable positions in a lot of ways.

Another participant provides a vivid example of porn-related abuse:

I think he's got a serious sick, sick problem. 'Cause he would laugh about it the next day. He would ejaculate in my hair, on my body. He would take certain clothes and clothing items out of the dresser if I wouldn't give him sex. He would, um, I don't know exactly what he did with it. He had this one real like, um, satiny spaghetti strap shirt and um, I found it between the bed and the box springs with a girly book, and a porn tape and it had cum all over it.

This woman also told DeKeseredy and Schwartz that her ex-partner watched porn "almost daily" and he would force her to watch it after he discovered that she wanted to leave him. She said, "Um, he'd put it in (a video) and he'd make me stay in the room with him while he watched it, while he was masturbating."

There is now quantitative evidence derived from a large-scale study—the NCVS—showing that rural women are at greater risk of being victims of intimate violence than their suburban and urban counterparts (Rennison, DeKeseredy, and Dragiewicz, 2012, 2013). DeKeseredy and Schwartz's (2009) study shows that pornography is certainly connected to rural woman abuse, and their study provides richer contextual data than the other two examined in this section. However, it is unclear why pornography is so closely related to male-to-female abuse in rural areas. Guided by DeKeseredy et al.'s (2014) research on rural pornography, we hypothesize that the strong association has something to do with the fact that despite, in general, being more politically conservative than metropolitan and suburban areas (Kay, 2011), rural communities, too, have become "pornified" (Paul, 2005). As Scott Bergthold, a U.S. lawyer who helps small town fight "adult business," told *Los Angeles Times* reporter Stephanie Simon (2004), "Rural communities never thought they'd have to deal with what they perceived to be a big-city problem" (p. 2). Obviously, things have changed, as "hard-core porn" has now hit the "heartland." For example, the Lion's Den chain now has an "adult superstore" in Quaker City, Ohio, population 563, because of its proximity to an interstate highway (Donnermeyer and DeKeseredy, 2014). In fact, at least a third of their stores are located off a U.S. interstate highway and in or near towns of 16,000 or fewer residents (Howlett, 2012). Also referred to as "freeway porn stores," Kat Sunlove, an adult porn star turned lobbyist working for the Free Speech Center, views these stores and the pornification of rural highways as "capitalism at its best . . . This is a transformed industry, and businesses are just following the market" (cited in Howlett, 2012, p. 1).

It is not only businesses that are following the market, but also rural consumers. For instance, there is now evidence that rural boys consume pornography more than do urban boys (Betowski, 2007; DeKeseredy and Olsson, 2011). Further, the states with the most pornographic subscription rates in the United States (e.g., Mississippi) have large rural populations (DeKeseredy et al., 2013; Edleman, 2009).

VIOLENCE AGAINST WOMEN IN THE PORNOGRAPHY INDUSTRY[6]

In Chapter 2, we briefly mentioned the pain and suffering experienced by many women in the porn industry. As Bridges and Anton (2013), among many others, remind us, one of the most well-known individuals who was hurt during the production of a porn film was Linda Lovelace, star of the 1972 movie Deep Throat.[7] During the making of this movie, her then husband Chuck Traynor imprisoned her and beat her. Actually, her marriage to this abusive man was riddled with violence and forced prostitution.[8] Yet, as exemplified in Box 4.1, her pain and suffering were frequently ridiculed in male bonding rituals. Box 4.1 begs this question: What is the value of allowing students to show and watch pornographic media on campus? In response to this question, some students who claim to be concerned about the financial well-being of student organizations, athletic teams, and other campus-based organizations contend that pornographic movies generate a substantial amount of money for these groups. For instance, according to Sanday (1996), in 1984, the University of Pennsylvania student organization that showed pornographic movies twice that year made $3000—more than it generated from any other business venture. But, for many people, Box 4.1 challenges the assertion that these films should be publicly screened on campus because they are profitable.

Are Lovelace's violent experiences common? This is a question that can only be answered empirically. Unfortunately, in-depth research on the abuse that women in the porn industry endure is in short supply. Still, some empirical work is available confirming that porn does considerable harm to women featured in it. For example, according to Bridges and Anton (2013), Grudzen et al. (2011) are the only researchers to have studied the psychological and physical abuse experienced by women in porn. The participants in their study were women porn performers based in California and their responses were compared to those of women of comparable age who participated in a larger state-wide health study. Grudzen et al. found that, compared to women in general, women in the porn industry:

- had 1.5 more poor mental health days;
- had three times more depressive disorders;
- were 1.5 times more likely to be currently living in poverty;
- were five times more likely to be survivors of domestic violence;

Box 4.1 THE SHOWING OF *DEEP THROAT* AT THE UNIVERSITY OF PENNSYLVANIA

Before the showing of *Deep Throat*, Linda Lovelace, its star, was brought by Penn's Women's Center to speak. Nearly two thousand people attended her talk. She spoke about her imprisonment during the making of the film, the beatings she suffered, and pointed out that the film shows the bruises on her body.

Two days later protestors, mostly female, and moviegoers, mostly male, showed up to see the film. The atmosphere was rowdy, and although it was against university rules, many males came carrying beer cans. Throughout the screening the voices of the film were drowned out by the constant din created by males chanting, "Bruises, bruises."

While waiting for the film to start, mindful of the protestors outside, men in the audience yelled, "We can have our fun," and "Hey, we're here to see Linda. We're going to love her bruises." A chant went up, "*Deep Throat, Deep Throat*, Let's go, Quakers, let's go." Men excitedly pointed to one another in the audience, yelling names and strutting around. "Hey, Smith, hey, Jones, what are you doing here?" "Psi Omega's here!!"

One man stood up and shouted, "Hey, you girls out there," referring to the protestors, "watch for the popcorn trick," referring to a movie in which a man sticks his erect penis in a popcorn box and offers popcorn to the woman next to him.

Once the movie started, the audience cheered and shouted, "Bruises, bruises" as Linda appeared on the screen in a short dress. Deep husky voices shouted, Blow job blow job," "Black leather," "Jerk off, jerk off!" The "bruises" refrain was especially deafening in those scenes where they were clearly visible. At one point, a man shouted, "Ugly bitch," and another added, "She's really ugly all over, including her bruises."

The audience cheered whenever Linda did a "deep throat" blow job. One man yelled, "Why can't my girlfriend do that?" During another blow job, a man screamed, "I'm *horny!!*" "Fuck her," another voice chimed in.

Almost all of the women present as spectators left the theater before the end of the film. The scene played out their worst fears of what getting caught in a locker room after a particularly nasty game and becoming the object of male wrath might be like.

After it was over, some of the protestors interviewed males as they left. The reaction they encountered was mixed. Some expressed little enthusiasm for the movie and admitted they wouldn't go to another porn film. One was disgusted by the whole scene, yet he felt it should be shown on campus. Another was bored, saying, "It makes sex very mechanical." Another male, a freshman, came up to the protestors and said in a coaxing tone, "Come on, she must have enjoyed some of that," referring to Linda Lovelace. "Look at her facial expressions. She never looked like she was upset. She had only one bruise on her thigh." He concluded, "I'd go to another porn film. It really looked like she was getting into it."

Source: Sanday (1996, p. 203–205).

- were roughly three times more likely to have been sexually abused as children;
- were two times more likely to have grown up in poverty; and
- were five times more likely to have been in foster care.

Below are data about the work-related health problems of women porn performers compared to women in the general population:

- only 10 percent of porn actresses consistently used condoms;
- porn actresses had eight times more sexual partners in the previous year;
- porn actresses were four times more likely to smoke cigarettes and twice as likely to drink alcohol;
- porn actresses were less likely to have health insurance; and
- they were more likely to be unable to meet their basic needs in the past 12 months.

These data reveal that there is nothing glamorous about being a "porn star." Recall, too, that in Chapter 2 we stressed that a woman's "choice" is often structured by "extremely limited options" (Corsianos, 2007, 2012) and violent childhood experiences (Boyle, 2011; Bridges and Anton, 2013). However, further in-depth quantitative and qualitative research on the damage done to women in the porn business is required to conclusively validate Grudzen et al.'s findings. More research is also needed on the relationship between pornography and human trafficking.

PORNOGRAPHIC CYBER-BULLYING[9]

The electronic and violent pornification of women and girls takes many different shapes and forms. One variant that is garnering more media and legal attention are behaviors such as the events of Steubenville, Ohio briefly described in Chapter 3. Referred to here as *pornographic cyber-bullying*, sometimes, as noted in Box 4.2, the consequences are deadly. Described in Box 4.2, the death of Rehtaeh Parsons on April 7, 2013 motivated the Canadian province of Nova Scotia to proclaim the Cyber-Safety Act on August 6, 2013. This law created Canada's first cyber-investigative unit and permits families and victims to get court protection orders. Additionally, school principals in Nova Scotia now have the explicit authority to act against cyber-bullying on and/or off school grounds and the legislation allows victims to sue alleged cyber-bullies.

Technological means of pornographic cyber-bullying have no time limits and many targets of such victimization are female adolescents like Rehtaeh Parsons. While this type of woman abuse varies, one of the most common means is "sexting." Consistent with what happened to Parsons, this involves sharing compromising photos, videos, or written information with other people via texts or other electronic media (Klein, 2013).

Box 4.2 REHTAEH PARSONS, CANADIAN GIRL DIES AFTER SUICIDE ATTEMPT; PARENTS ALLEGE SHE WAS RAPED BY FOUR BOYS

A 17-year-old Canadian girl died Sunday following a suicide attempt last week. The family of Rehtaeh Parsons said their daughter never recovered from an alleged rape by four teenage boys in November 2011 that left her deeply depressed and rejected by her community.

Placed on life support last Thursday at a local hospital, Rehtaeh Parsons died on April 7 after her family made the decision to take her off life support.

In a Facebook memorial page, the girl's mother, Leah Parsons, wrote that Rehtaeh had been shunned and harassed after one of the boys allegedly involved in the rape took a picture of the incident and distributed it to their "school and community, where it quickly went viral."

"Rehtaeh is gone today because of the four boys that thought raping a 15-year-old girl was okay, and to distribute a photo to ruin her spirit and reputation would be fun," Parsons wrote.

According to Canadian news outlet CBC, the alleged sexual assault happened at a small gathering at which teenagers consumed alcohol. One of the boys in attendance reportedly took a photo of another boy having sex with Rehtaeh Parsons and sent it to friends.

Gawker writes that the bullying got so bad after the photo circulated that the family was forced to relocate.[10]

"She was never left alone. She had to leave the community. Her friends turned against her. People harassed her. Boys she didn't know started texting her and Facebooking her asking her to have sex with them. It just never stopped." Leah Parsons told the CBC.

As described by Parson, the shaming and harassment stemming from the incident had long-lasting psychological and emotional effects on her daughter. Parsons told Maritime Noon[11] that Rehtaeh suffered from depression and had checked herself into a hospital after having suicidal thoughts last March. A Twitter account that appears to have belonged to Parsons features references to drug culture, as well as what appears to be drug paraphernalia.

Source: *Huffington Post* (2014, p. 1).

The damage caused by behaviors like "sexting" is lifelong. This warning by the National Campaign to Prevent Teen Pregnancy and Unplanned Pregnancy and CosmoGirl.Com (2012) spells out the danger:

There is no changing your mind in cyberspace—anything you send or post will never truly go away. Something that seems fun and flirty and is done on a whim will never really die. Potential employers, college recruiters, teachers, coaches, parents, friends, enemies, strangers, and others may all be able to find your past posts, even after you delete them. And it is nearly impossible to control what other people are posting about you. Think about it: Even if you have second thoughts and delete a racy photo, there is no telling who has already copied that photo and posted it elsewhere.

(p. 2)

Keep in mind the statistics below generated by a national U.S. survey conducted by the aforementioned two organizations:

- 38 percent of teen girls and 39 percent of teen boys say they have had sexually suggestive text messages or emails—originally meant for someone else shared with them.
- 25 percent of teen girls and 33 percent of teen boys say they have had nude or seminude images—originally meant for someone else—shared with them.
- 37 percent of young adult women and 47 percent of young adult men have had sexually suggestive text messages or emails—intended for someone else—shared with them.
- 24 percent of young adult women and 40 percent of young adult men say they have had nude or seminude images—originally meant for someone else—shared with them.

(p. 3)

It is obvious by now that pornographic cyber-bullying causes many physical and psychological problems and the death of Rehtaeh Parsons is now commonly termed as "cyberbullicide" (Hinduja and Patchin, 2009). In a study of 1,963 U.S. middle schoolers, Hindjua and Patchin (2010) found that victims of various kinds of cyber-bullying were more likely to have suicidal thoughts and to have made suicide attempts. Of course, there is no way of knowing how many students succeeded in these attempts (since this was a survey of school students). Even so, they argue that these extreme reactions require the need for vigilance on the part of school officials and the government of Nova Scotia strongly agrees. All too often, however, school officials and even criminal justice officials do not take cyber-bullying seriously (DeKeseredy and Schwartz, 2013; Klein, 2012).

To a large extent, *revenge pornography* websites and blogs are forms of pornographic cyber-bullying. Actually, it is estimated that there are now more than 2,000 such sites and the bulk of the perpetrators are male (Hart, 2014). Revenge porn images and videos are made by men with the consent of the women they were intimately involved with, but then distributed online without their consent typically following the termination of a relationship. The harm done by revenge porn is irreparable, but the criminal justice system's response has been woefully inadequate (Salter and Crofts, 2014) until recently. In December 2014, Noe Iniguez, 36, of Los Angeles became the first person to be convicted under California's "revenge porn" law. The man who posted nude photos of his ex-girlfriend without her consent on her employer's Facebook page was sentenced to one year in jail and 36 months of probation, and will be required to attend domestic violence counseling for violating both the state's revenge porn statute and two restraining orders. California was the first state to adopt "revenge porn" legislation in October 2013; and, since then, more than a dozen states have passed similar laws (O'Connor, 2014).

We could easily provide many more examples of pornographic cyber-bullying. But, to make matters worse, many adults are completely unaware of what is going on in the dark side of the Internet and other new media (Dines, 2010). With the constant stream of new technologies and new "apps," it is easy for gender-related harms inflicted by some new technologies to go unnoticed. For instance, in the Fall of 2014, at Corsianos' institution, Eastern Michigan University, three women professors had no idea they were under attack by students in their class who were posting remarks anonymously via Yik Yak (a new smartphone application) until one of their students approached them after class with the evidence. According to the *Chronicle of Higher Education*, since the release of this application in November 2013, Yik Yak has "been causing havoc on campuses as a result of students' posting threats of harm, racial slurs, and slanderous gossip" (Schmidt, 2015). In the case of EMU, students had written more than 100 demeaning Yik Yak posts about the women, including sexual remarks, insults about their appearances, and derogatory terms for women, and for female anatomy. This, as well as other similar Yik Yak attacks, were also later reported by the New York Times.[12]

We, like many other scholars, activists, and practitioners, agree with this observation made by Vargas-Martin, Garcia-Ruiz, and Edwards (2011):

> While the future will surely bring new developments and technological applications, we, technology savvy professionals, need to continue developing new ways [and] better policies ... to use technology for the benefit of humanity while determining misuses and promoting best practices.

> (p. xxvii)

NEW DIRECTIONS IN RESEARCH[13]

Again, we know that pornography consumption is correlated with violence against women, but new empirical advances are necessary to enhance a social scientific understanding of this relationship. For example, as far as we know, no one has followed in DeKeseredy and Schwartz's (1998a) footsteps and conducted another national representative sample survey of how porn is connected to violence against adult women. This is partly a function of government agencies' inability or unwillingness to fund such a project. Note, too, that conducting research on how porn influences the abuse of adult women does not appear to be a top priority for many, if not most, North American domestic violence coalitions. As well, the general population does not appear keen to empirically ask questions about porn. Note, too, that over the past 25 years, pornography has "even been a divisive issue among people who call themselves feminist" (Katz, 2006, p. 185).

More survey research is definitely needed. So are life-course studies. Life course theories and research are popular among mainstream criminological circles (e.g., Laud and Sampson, 2003; Sampson and Laub, 1993). Following Glen Elder (1994), the life course is defined here as "the interweave of age-graded trajectories, such as work careers and family pathways, that are subject to changing conditions and future options, and to short-term transitions ranging from leaving school to retirement" (p. 5). The life course perspective has not penetrated the realm of pornography empirical and theoretical work, but applying it to this field of study allows for a richer understanding of using pornography, porn's relationship to violence, and the continuation or termination of porn use across the lifespan (LeBlanc and Loeber, 1998; Piquero and Mazerolle, 2001).

Many questions about pornography and its role in violence against women are difficult or impossible to answer with anonymous, self-report questionnaires given one time, in one place, to one group of people. This "one shot" approach is excellent for documenting the correlation between porn use and male-to-female violence. Like scores of studies of street youth gang membership, however, they tell us little, if anything, about the trajectory of individuals who use porn. Life-course research has another benefit. Many critics have argued that surveys can misrepresent people or be misinterpreted. A longitudinal study that examines a large number of men over a long period of time with multiple measures of male porn use mitigates many of these criticisms. Further, the validity of theoretical constructs is strengthened (White and Humphrey, 1997).

Another refreshing alternative to simply using cross-sectional survey research is participant observation, a technique that dominates male peer support research. In fact, two male peer support theories of woman abuse developed by DeKeseredy and Schwartz (see DeKeseredy, 1988; DeKeseredy and Schwartz 1993) were heavily informed by observational studies of patriarchal pub dynamics (Hey, 1986; Whitehead, 1976); combative sports teams (Young, 1988), and fraternities (1990). We have presented some scholars' (e.g., Kimmel, 2008; Sanday, 1996) observations of men in groups consuming porn in several sections of this book, but at the time we completed writing this book in the summer of 2014, no one had published an in-depth ethnographic account of men's porn use and its effects on their behavior.

It is important to embrace multiple ways of knowing and not to be wedded to any particular method. Certainly, the techniques briefly suggested here constitute just the tip of the iceberg. Indeed, there are many more such as archival research. Regardless of which piece of the pornography and violence against women puzzle a researcher wants to study, though, he or she should strive for "data triangulation" (Denzin, 1978). As Denzin and Lincoln (2005) put it, "The combination of multiple methodological practices, empirical materials, perspectives, and observers in a single study is best understood, then, as a strategy that adds rigor, breadth, complexity, richness, and depth to any study" (p. 5). Like a civil engineer, using a variety of "sightings" for different angles makes it more likely that we will correctly survey the "dark side" of male's consumption of sexual materials (Fielding and Fielding, 1986).

It isn't only new empirical work that is needed. Most of the research on pornography, especially the quantitative work done in labs, is atheoretical or characterized by "abstracted empiricism" (e.g., research divorced from theory) (Mills, 1959; Young, 2011). New theories need to be developed and tested because, as stated in Chapter 3, social scientific theories of pornography use and its effects are in short supply. Theories are not "just fanciful ideas that have little to do with what truly motivates people" (Akers and Sellers, 2013, p. 1). Rather, as stated by Kurt Lewin (1951), the founder of modern social psychology, "There is nothing so practical as good theory" (p. 169). Undoubtedly, if we hope to prevent violence against women and other hurtful symptoms of broader patriarchal forces, we have to move beyond doing simply correlational research and provide empirically informed answers to questions such as those raised by Jackson Katz (2006):

■ How does heterosexual men's use of pornography as a masturbatory aid help to shape not only their view of women and girls, but also their own manhood and sexuality?
■ What is the influence on boy's sexuality of early and repeated exposure to the pornography's industry's particular representation of "normal sex?"
■ What is the relationship between the sexual abuse of children and the proliferation of media products that deliberately sexualize young girls—and in some cases boys?
■ What can be done about what seems to be a steady movement away from the idea of sex as mutually respectful?

(p. 182)

SUMMARY

The above section ended with some "uncomfortable questions, and what makes them even more difficult is that not everyone wants to know the answers" (Katz, 2006, p. 182). Fortunately, the leading anti-pornography scholars in the field continue to make those who consume and produce degrading, racist, and violent sexual media uncomfortable. Yet, there is much more work to be done and an integral part of the movement to recognize and counter violent and abusive pornography is high quality research documenting the correlation between hurtful sexual media and violence against women. Then again, it is time to move beyond going down the "well-trodden path" of conducting highly problematic laboratory studies (Ferrell, Hayward, and Young, 2008). It is often stated that lab research overstates the connection between porn and various types of woman abuse, but there is ample evidence supporting Jensen's (2003) claim that "we should be at least as concerned that lab studies underestimate pornography's role in promoting misogynistic attitudes and behavior. . . ." (p. 418).

There are excellent alternatives to lab studies, such as surveys done by feminist scholars like Russell (1990). Additionally, feminist research involving in-depth interviews with men and women glean rich, insightful information that can never be obtained in a lab (e.g., Jensen, 1995, 1996; Kelly, 1988). And, the new directions in empirical work suggested previously are destined to provide detailed answers to questions such as Katz's (2006). Regardless of which method is used, while it is impossible to prove that any type of pornography *causes* violence against women (Boyle, 2003), we do know that there is a very close relationship between these two factors and that pornography is increasingly shaping many men's sexual behaviors (Jensen, 2003). Sadly, as Katz (2006) puts it, "some men's sexual pleasure is actually enhanced by the mistreatment and degradation of women" (p. 189).

Pornography and misogyny are inextricably linked and we should heed the words of U.S. journalist Bob Herbert (2009): "We would become much more sane, much healthier, as a society if we could bring ourselves to acknowledge that misogyny is a serious and pervasive problem, and the twisted way so many men feel about women . . . is a toxic mix of the most tragic proportions" (p. 1). What is to be done? How do we create a healthier society? In Chapter 5 we provide progressive answers to these questions.

DISCUSSION QUESTIONS

1. What are the criticisms made against studies that attempt to show a cause-and-effect relationship between viewing violent porn and committing violent sexual acts?
2. What do we learn from feminist research on hurtful sexual media and violence against women?
3. Why do you think there hasn't been another national survey since DeKeseredy and Schwartz's 1998 study on how porn is connected to violence against women?

NOTES

1. This section includes revised material published previously by DeKeseredy and Schwartz (1998a, 2009, 20013) and Schwartz and DeKeseredy (1998).
2. This section includes modified sections of work published previously by DeKeseredy and Schwartz (1998a) and Schwartz and DeKeseredy (1998).
3. See, for example, Attwood (2010b), Lehman (2006b), and McNair (2002).
4. This section includes modified parts of work published previously by DeKeseredy and Schwartz (2013).
5. This section includes material adapted from work published earlier by DeKeseredy et al. (2013) and Donnermeyer and DeKeseredy (2014).
6. This section includes modified parts of work published previously by DeKeseredy and Schwartz (1998a).
7. Her real name was Linda Susan Boreman and she died in 2002.
8. See her 1979 book *Ordeal: The Truth Behind Deep Throat* for more information on the abuse she endured.

9. This section includes revised material published earlier by DeKeseredy and Schwartz (2013).
10. *Gawker* is a blog that proclaims itself as "the source for daily Manhattan media news and gossip." It includes stories about celebrities and the media industry.
11. Maritime Noon is a Canadian Broadcasting Corporation (CBC) radio news show that is broadcasted to the provinces of New Brunswick, Nova Scotia, and Prince Edward Island.
12. See New York Times article by Jonathan Mahler (MARCH 8, 2015) Who Spewed That Abuse? Anonymous Yik Yak App Isn't Telling www.nytimes.com/2015/03/09/technology/popular-yik-yak-app-confers-anonymity-and-delivers-abuse.html?_r=0
13. This section includes revised work published previously by DeKeseredy and Schwartz (1998b, 2013).

Chapter 5

Challenging Porn
Progressive Policy Proposals

We need to offer an alternative way of being, a way to envisage a sexuality that is based on equality, dignity, and respect. Part of this inevitably means organizing against the commodification of human needs and desires.

(Dines, 2010, p. 164)

THE mainstreaming of violence in today's pornography must be recognized and challenged. As discussed in previous chapters, violent and degrading images in porn have become commonplace which serve to further strengthen the current misogynistic climate; both its messages and practices. Individuals, groups, and organizations must commit to raising public awareness of the consequences of this porn culture. For Andrea Dworkin and Catharine MacKinnon, "porn is not what it says but what it does". We must constantly raise the questions "who is writing the vast majority of pornographic scripts?" and "who is their intended audience?" As discussed earlier, most porn is created typically by straight, white males for largely a straight white male audience, and therefore, the question that must constantly be interrogated is whether women can have agency in their sexual lives when they live in a porn culture where patriarchal, and heterosexist images of human bodies are the norm, and include hypermasculinized male sexual performances with various levels of aggression and violence against female sex partners.

The expression of sexual agency requires individuals to have the ability to evaluate sexual choices including one's own sexual identity. This includes making one's own choices in terms of sexual acts free of coercion, force, or conformity to external social norms (Corsianos, 2007). But, how can "sexual agency" be made possible in an environment where misogynistic images of women have become commodified, commercialized, and popularized in the cultural imagination?

According to Catharine MacKinnon and Andrea Dworkin, agency can only be located in resistance to porn. MacKinnon (1993) asserts that: "With pornography, men masturbate to women being exposed, humiliated, violated, degraded, mutilated, dismembered, bound, gagged, tortured, and killed. In the visual materials, they experience this *being done* by watching it *being done*. What is real here is not that the materials are pictures, but that they are part of a sex act" (p. 101).

Similarly, for Gail Dines (2010) the current porn culture must be stopped. As she puts it,

> the most obvious technique that the pornographers employ here is to verbally segregate this group of women by calling them cunts, whores, sluts, cum-dumpsters, beavers, and so on. . . . In porn, sex is framed as not just consensual but as something that the woman seeks out because she loves to be sexually used. This also is a method for lessening any guilt the user may feel as he can reassure himself that she is not being hurt, or if she is, it is what she wants.
>
> (p. 64)

On the other hand, others have claimed to challenge mainstream misogynistic images in porn by attempting to redefine some of porn's dominant's scripts. For example, Candida Royalle (2000) has aimed to challenge these images and performances in an attempt to create necessary social spaces for straight women's sexual agency. She produces pornographic films that are aimed at straight women and opposite-sex couples. Royalle (2000) asserts:

> I wanted to make films that made people feel good about their sexuality and about who they are as sexual beings. I wanted to make films that say we all have the right to pleasure, and that women, especially, have a right to our own pleasure.
>
> (p. 543)

Also, Louise Lush (2013), who along with about twenty other women formed the Women's Erotica Network (WEN), described her early work in making porn for women as follows: "We were essentially making up the concept of porn for women as we went along. There wasn't much to go on; we really only had the films of Candida Royalle and the male centerfolds of Playgirl as a guide, as well as our own ideas of what was sexy" (p. 73). She defines "good porn for women" as involving the "depiction of sex where the woman's pleasure is paramount. It has to be about HER experience of sex, HER pleasure, and HER orgasm. Everything else is really just window dressing" (p. 74). But, despite this view, she recognizes that it is:

> difficult to source erotic material that fits the bill. Straight women complain that they can't find good porn. Women are still on the outside. The box covers of straight adult DVDs all feature photos of women, not men. A search of "porn" still brings us hundreds of mainstream websites, most of which talk about "shooting your load" and "your cock" rather than "your clit.". . . . And most of them finish with a male orgasm, often without bothering to feature a female orgasm.
>
> (p. 77)

And, for feminist porn star and performance artist Dylan Ryan (2013), making what she calls "authentic" porn means prioritizing her sexuality. Recasting the dominant images of porn is one of her main goals and she credits self-defined feminist pornographers such as Tristan Taormino as an adult-film trailblazer for challenging dominant porn scripts. Examples include female domination and the recent emergence of "pegging", where women anally penetrate men.

Similarly, Salaman (1993) has pushed for increased availability of pornography produced by women for women. But, some self-defined feminist pornographers depict women who are hog-tied while having sex that looks painful, or women who are suspended from the ceiling while men penetrate them. They argue that some women are turned on by being submissive and therefore that needs to be respected. What makes their work "feminist", they claim, is that the actors work in a safe working environment and the actors are asked what kinds of sex acts they want to participate in, whereas in mainstream porn, performers are not given a choice. Also, they claim "feminist" porn features actors who are more diverse in age, size, race, and sexual orientation than in mainstream pornographic movies.

But, a key question that has been raised by various academics and activists is whether women can experience "sexual agency" when they appropriate patriarchal and hetero-normative definitions of sexual performances of female bodies as promoted in mainstream porn. For instance, Julia Penelope (1992) in responding to the appropriation of patriarchal gendered performances by lesbians asserts that:

> those aspects of behavior and appearance labeled "femininity" in HP [heteropatriarchy] are dangerous to us. We still live in a HP and Lesbians who incorporate male ideas of appropriate female behaviors into their lives signal their acceptance of the HP version of reality.
>
> (p. 81)

Similarly, Janice Raymond (1989) notes:

> It is difficult to see what is so advanced or progressive about a position that locates "desire", and that imprisons female sexual dynamics, vitality, and vigor, in old forms of sexual objectification, subordination, and violence, this time initiated by women and done with women's consent.
>
> (p. 149)

Also, in response to self-defined feminist pornographer Tristan Taormino, Gail Dines does not view anything empowering in Taormino's work or other self-defined feminist pornographers who depict violent sex acts against women regardless of whether they're being done by women or men.

There is no denying the influences of dominant social forces in the sexual lives of people. Indeed, individuals are unique, but, are at the same time products of their culture (Griswold, 1986). Individuals have their own personality which refers to the fairly consistent patterns of acting, thinking and feeling, but, personality is largely the result of socialization. As sociologists assert, nurture/socialization is humanity's nature. Without socialization, people cannot mature intellectually, socially, emotionally, and psychologically (Begley, 1995; Goldsmith, 1983; Mead, 1962, orig. 1934). People continuously "take in"/internalize what they see, hear, and read and make decisions with respects to how they should act, think, and feel about different things. And, as Simone DeBeauvoir stated, "One is not born a woman, but rather, becomes a woman." People are social creatures continuously shaped and influenced by external social forces, and given the undeniable presence and accessibility of misogynistic porn in our society today, we cannot ignore the ways these popularized commodified images impact people's perceptions of "women," "men," sex, sexuality, violence, and relationships. For Butler (1997):

> to be a woman is to have become a woman, to compel the body to conform to an historical ideal of "woman," to induce the body to become a cultural sign, to materialize oneself in obedience to an historically delimited possibility, and to do this as a sustained and repeated corporeal project . . . indeed, those who fail to do their gender right are regularly punished. Because there is neither an "essence" that gender expresses or externalizes nor an objective idea to which gender aspires; because gender is not a fact, the various acts of gender creates the idea of gender, and without those acts, there would be no gender at all. Gender is, thus, a construction that regularly conceals its genesis.
>
> (pp. 404–405)

The body becomes its gender through a series of acts which are renewed and revised over time. In the current world of Internet porn, to assume there are no real-world consequences is not only naïve but dangerous. Indeed, both "women" and "men" are oppressed sexually by the porn industry, but the consequences to their oppressions are not the same given society's dominant patriarchal social forces that privilege males over females. At the same time, one cannot assert that all "women" who live in a society where pornography has become commonplace personally experience the same kinds of sexual oppressions, but, we can certainly identify "oppressive" experiences they all share whether consciously recognized or not. Sexual oppression here refers to the denial of sexual agency and include instances where women feel that their sexual selves are confined within a set of parameters, do not recognize other potential possibilities relating to their sexual lives, are denied a voice or opportunity to express their sexual selves, are pressured to engage in sex acts that hurt them or make them feel uncomfortable, and/or are subjected to negative attitudes, ideas or acts for challenging the status quo. An experience can still be considered "oppressive" even if not recognized by the individual as such because there are consequences to that oppression (e.g., not having the freedom to experience sex differently whether physically, emotionally, and/or psychologically, being limited to particular self-sexual identities, performing in uncomfortable, or objectionable ways to be sexually desired). These "effects" impact women's lives whether or not they recognize the influencing factors of the cause of the experience(s). For Corsianos (2012), gender differences can be understood relationally and situationally and regardless of differences in the experiences of "women"—whether they are women of color, straight women, lesbians, mothers, white women, minority ethnic women, etc. they have at various levels been denied sexual agency because of this socially-constructed category of "woman" or "women." As representations of these social categories and living in a culture that promotes pornography and the mainstreaming of violence, "women" experience forms of "oppression" directly and/or indirectly, whether consciously recognized or not, in the values, attitudes, language, images, and physical actions represented in dominant organizational structures and social systems. The category "woman" or "women" continues to be shaped and influenced by patriarchal and heterosexist social forces (Corsianos, 2011; 2009).

Regardless of how different people's personal experiences may be in how they view themselves sexually, the choices they make about their sexual lives are governed by societal expectations of gender normative behavior. For others, who have rejected these dominant constructed "truths", they too have experienced consequences whether they are aware of them or not, and therefore, share similarities in experience. These realities have consequences in the lives of all "women". But, as people are inundated by hegemonic (Connell, 2005; Gramsci, 1957; Messerschmidt, 2003) social forces, it becomes difficult to see how the above mentioned "truths" affect individuals' lives directly and/or indirectly. Many people consent to the dominant ideologies because they are made to feel that these values, practices, and images somehow reflect their personal interests. This, in part, offers some insight into the public's tolerance of the images/products produced by the porn industry.

We must not forget that even the steps taken to strive to promote gender equality and non-heterosexist perspectives are produced within a society whereby dominant ideologies are so pervasive, so internalized that they render many unable to envision the possibilities for sexual agency. Also, many are not only unaware of the origins of the politics of the gendered body, but as mentioned above, often assume sexual "choices" are made on an individual level regardless of external pressures. For Miller-Young (2013):

> though feminism seeks to dismantle structural and discursive exploitation and oppression of women and marginalized populations, our feminist praxis is not external to or untouched by hegemonic systems of domination. Theorizing a feminist pornography then means thinking about a dual process of transgression and restriction, for both representation and labor.
>
> (p. 107)

To promote independent sexual subjectivity there must be opportunity to challenge the status quo where sexual expression is concerned in order to make informed decisions about self-definitions of sexual identities. What must change is the very foundation of the social order to attain a semblance of equality (Corsianos, 2000) in order to have the ability to be in sexual relationships based on respect and dignity.

The current gender and sexuality hierarchy must be challenged and a redefinition of the current social order is required to challenge dominant sexual ideologies and enable people to make meaningful sexual choices. Only in a non-patriarchal and non-heterosexist society where assumptions about identity categories such as "woman" and "man" "straight", "lesbian", "bisexual" cease to exist, and where "femininity" and "masculinity" are no longer defined and valued in hierarchical ways and assumed to be tied to a particular sex, can sexual agency become possible.

In a society that promotes gender equality, there would not be a monopoly on particular sexual images and sexual performances, and violence would not be integrated in sex acts. We could then celebrate the diverse eclectic images of human bodies as both sexual and asexual beings, and sexual performances based on dignity and respect would be made possible.

But, the movement must also include men because they too are dehumanized by porn and turned into one-dimensional objects. Indeed, they are often in positions of power in much of the mainstream porn but these images teach men what they need to "do" to be sexually accepted, to be seen as desirable and masculine. As discussed earlier, men are not oppressed in the same ways, but given how the porn industry creates "hypermasculinized" sexual images of straight men who must perform like machines, maintain an erection at all times, have an above-average penis size, and be always in control of the woman or women in the sex act, there is no denying the insecurities and vulnerabilities these create in men. For Dines (2010), "What resistance to porn offers men is a sexuality that celebrates connectedness, intimacy, and empathy—a sexuality bathed in equality rather than subordination" (p. 165). Also, she argues that "Women and men must throw these industrial images out of our bedrooms and our heads so that we can develop a way of being sexual that does not dictate conformity to the plasticized, generic, and formulaic sex on offer in a porn culture. Such a sexuality cannot be scripted by a movement because it belongs to individuals and reflects who they are and what they want sexually" (p. 164).

We are at a crucial point in time given the increased demand for more extreme, violent, and degrading porn. Both government and the mainstream media must be held accountable and begin a national conversation on porn as a social problem and recognize that criminal acts are being committed. With the mainstreaming of violence in porn, we can no longer afford to not pay attention. The government and the mainstream media often work together to socially construct issues as "problems". As Philip Jenkins (2009) asserts:

> society cannot panic about everything at once, and some issues must therefore take a subordinate role to others. But some issues just seem just so naturally tempting that it is difficult to understand their absence from centre-stage.
> (p. 36)

So, why hasn't there been a public outcry about the level of violence in today's porn? Why hasn't there been a "moral panic" created as seen, for instance, in the "get tough on crime" government policies and the media's reporting of female violent offenders?

Interestingly, females commit fewer crimes in comparison to males, and despite early "liberation" theorists, the rate of women's criminal offending is significantly lower in comparison to males, and the actual criminal behaviors reveal gendered patterns (Chesney-Lind and Shelden, 1992; Flavin, 2001; Morris, 1987; Naffine, 1996; 1987; Smart, 1982). But, despite this information, the mainstream media chooses to sensationalize particular crimes involving female suspects particularly when the crimes are excessively violent and provide "sensational" appeal (Belknap, 2007), and government policies have supported more punitive measures for offenders. The constant reporting of violent female "criminals" creates a "moral panic"; it is assumed that violent criminal offending by women is rampant, and has become an "epidemic" of sorts. On the other hand, the violence and brutality promoted in porn and the crimes being committed by the porn industry have gone unnoticed.

Mainstream crime news focuses on the sensational and the unusual often reinforcing biases and stereotypes (Faith, 1987; McCormick, 1995; Mills, 1990;). The news stories are typically not educational; they do not inform the public about the various serious implications of crimes. For Kurtz (1994), and McCormick (1995), features of mainstream crime news reporting include sensationalism and "entertainment". This way the probability of capturing the attention of the public is increased by strategically providing all the lurid details with the traditional voyeurism of crime news reporting. But, at the same time, crime news stories must have "legitimate" victims as perceived by mainstream society.

For instance, in Corsianos (2012), despite the frequency of police criminality, only particular types of police corruption cases were deemed "newsworthy" by the mainstream media and yet other forms of abuses were condoned and/or entirely not recognized which served as evidence of hegemonic masculinity in policing in how particular forms of violence were "naturalized" and in the sense of entitlement, "brotherhood," secrecy, and autonomy that exists among police officers. Also, reported police corruption cases included "legitimate" victims. In other words, police were less likely to be concerned about possible police abuses involving individuals who would not be deemed "legitimate" by the wider public; this included the poor, the homeless, sex workers, drug users, and persons with prior criminal records.

With regards to reporting the actions of the porn industry however, the mainstream media has, with few exceptions, remained silent. When they actually discuss porn it is typically glamorized. (However, working with the mainstream media is an important component to raising awareness and suggestions on how to work with the mainstream media will be provided further down). And, as discussed in Chapter 2, police involvement in adult pornography has been largely non-existent.

The police and news organizations must maintain a close working relationship. Police agencies are the primary suppliers of crime stories in general, and, over time, the police as a "credible" source have become conventional wisdom (Ericson, 1989; Fishman, 1981). The relationship can be described as one of "give and take." Police have access to a "crime story" that they make available to the media, but, at the same time they control how the incident is framed. For Sacco (1995), the crime story "must be viewed as serious enough and as visual enough to be chosen over competing issues" (p. 172). But, the police, as the mainstream media, fail to view the serious implications of today's porn industry.

Interestingly, with regards to Internet child porn specifically, Philip Jenkins (2009) asserts that it has every qualification to become the basis of a moral panic. "The underlying situation is large-scale, and can easily be portrayed as threatening particularly as it affects children. It is also undergoing rapid expansion, as the Internet further extends its hegemony over global commerce and communication" (p. 37). But, he argues that there are several reasons why Internet child porn has not been prioritized by the media; one of which is technological. "Most law-enforcement agencies work at a technological level that is simply too low to comprehend the trade as it actually existed a decade ago, and still less today. They have little idea of the nature of the trade, its complex world of concealment and deception through proxies and anonymizers" (p. 38). According to Philip Jensen, there's been a "failure to launch" child porn into a moral panic because of the lack of technological understanding on the part of law enforcement, the lack of media access since journalistic access to original material is entirely forbidden, and the invisibility of the problem since the material typically cannot simply be "stumbled upon." But, this is very different from the overwhelming availability and accessibility of adult violent pornography and porn that "claims" to present actors of legal age. So why is this porn not prioritized? Images of violence against women in porn are readily available and anyone with Internet access can view them from anywhere in the world and at any time. So why hasn't there been a public outcry?

Part of the reason, as mentioned earlier, is that hegemomic forces convince viewers that these images somehow reflect their personal interests. But, also, a common perception is that this is "just fantasy" with no real-world consequences. And, as mentioned above, when the porn industry is actually discussed by mainstream news organizations, it is often presented as "glamorous" and chic. For example, when Dines (2010) was invited as a guest on *Rita Cosby: Live and Direct* to talk about pornography, she described her experience as follows:

> The stage was set for a "nonjudgmental" show that in the end turned out to be an hour's advertisement of the porn industry. Making no attempt to explore the range of genre in porn, Cosby focused only on the feature side, and for the first 50 minutes most of the people she interviewed were connected to Vivid. I appeared in the last 10 minutes but was quickly silenced when I said that the show was an example of shoddy journalism as it promoted only a positive image of the porn industry.
>
> (p. 42)

The mainstream media serve as powerful vehicles for the dissemination of pro-porn ideology highlighting glamorous, chic images of porn stars. More recently, in March 2014 on CNN's Piers Morgan Tonight, a Duke University student was invited to talk about how porn empowers her and how she started doing porn to pay for college tuition. Absent was any educational awareness of the probability of crimes being committed by the porn industry which includes sexual assaults against women who are either forced or coerced to make videos/films and/or women who are physically assaulted, beaten and/or tortured during sex acts. Nor was there any meaningful discussion of the economic exploitation of performers, as well as health concerns relating to STDs and lack of heath care insurance. Rather, the focus of the show was how "doing porn" was sexually liberating for this Duke freshman who decided to come out and identify herself only after being "outed" by a fellow classmate to other Duke students. Stephanie Williams (2014) in an article in the *Huffington Post* titled "Belle Knox's Porn Crusade is Fantasy, Not Feminist" provided a refreshing response. She said:

> no young girls should be duped into believing that Belle Knox's experiences —whether they're legit or just a fantasy she's made up to try to counter the overwhelming and in most cases undeserved criticism she's faced—are the norm in the porn industry. The truth is there is a huge likelihood that young women who start doing porn will end up in a situation they don't want to be in, whether it's agreeing to perform an act they never wanted to perform, testing positive for an STD, getting introduced to drugs or being told to work for their part by servicing a director or agent. That's the reality of porn. Is it the reality for every girl? Probably not. Is it the reality for the majority? I'd bet a lot of money on it. But Belle Knox seems either blissfully unaware of this reality or in complete denial of it.

In instances where porn is likely to be viewed as violent, extreme, or degrading by the public, the material is still perceived to be without "legitimate" victims because of the level of victim blaming. The women are seen as "consenting"; putting themselves in positions of risk, wanting/desiring to be treated in violent ways. And, it is assumed that they are all free agents, participating by choice. The possibility of women being forced, or coerced is absent on the part of the mainstream media, and many in the wider public. But, this is not entirely surprising given how violence against women is condoned in other areas (e.g., in the home, in dating relationships, on the streets, in war, in prisons, and, in advertising and mainstream movies), and how the image of "crime" is socially constructed.

The porn industry demarcates women in porn not as "victims" but as "sluts" or "whores" who are deserving of what happens to them, and the probability that crimes are being committed is not recognized. Also, "crimes" have for the most part been constructed as being largely street-level crimes; this is where "danger" lies (Corsianos, 2012; 2011; 2001). And police resources reflect this. Police are not proactively policing obscenity laws nor do they investigate porn companies to determine whether actors' "participation" was coerced or forced, or whether they were physically assaulted during sex and therefore make arrests for sexual and aggravated assault. Any police work in this area is typically reactive; police investigations in the violation of obscenity laws are extremely rare as seen in Chapter 2.

Indeed, police do not serve "society" or "the people", but rather "some" parts of society and "some people" at the expense of others (Black, 1990; Corsianos, 2012; 2001; McLaughlin, 2007). Policing translates, as Ericson (1982) noted to "patrolling the petty." Police largely view "crimes" as those that are committed "on the streets" (e.g., drug use, stranger assaults, prostitution, theft, etc.). And, therefore, the image of "the criminal" is largely tied to class and 'race' identities given the types of crimes that are disproportionately committed by poorer people and racial minorities, and disproportionately policed. "Street-crimes," also referred to as "blue-collar crimes" are often visible and the police can intervene to make arrests. But, white-collar or corporate crimes including the crimes committed by the porn industry that affect everyone on some level are virtually condoned.

Also, police typically lack the resources, training, and knowledge to police obscenity laws and the porn industry. The police overwhelmingly protect those in privileged positions (Gordon, 1987; Neugebauer, 1999; 1996) which includes the lucrative porn industry and its alliances with large, mainstream corporations (Boyle, 2010; Jensen, 2007), and apply selective law enforcement to those who are economically and socially marginalized (Ericson, 1982; Gordon, 1987; Reiman and Leighton, 2010). As a result, grass-roots organizing must include raising public awareness of the roles of the police to date. Police priorities must be changed and the image of crime must include the harms done by the porn industry.

And in addition to increasing accountability on the part of the police, other avenues must be explored from working with the mainstream media and music industry, utilizing social media, creating school-based initiatives, and recognizing violence against women as a human rights issue.

WORKING WITH MAINSTREAM MEDIA

Patriarchal messages transmitted by the mainstream media and music industry tend to increase people's tolerance for sexist discourses and practices including violence against women. For instance, gangsta rap, a type of music with broad appeal among college/university students and other youth, sends out strong negative messages about the way to treat women and the need for an abusive patriarchal masculinity. Relationships are also characterized in many gangsta rap songs as unions in which men must dominate and control women. Females, too, are frequently referred to in numerous rap lyrics as "bitches" and "hoes." Some journalists, though, assert that rap artist Eminem and others who write and sing songs like this are creative. On the other hand, many feminists define these "musicians" as promoters of "hate humor" (Katz, 2006). It is easy to agree with this claim after hearing Eminem sing, "Put anthrax on your Tampax and slap you till you can't stand" (cited in Katz, 2006, p. 159).

African-American feminist Patricia Hill Collins (2000) sees rap as one of the contemporary "controlling images" used to oppress black women, and Oliver (2006) contends that rap's patriarchal or sexist lyrics offer justification for engaging in abusive acts against women of color. Nonetheless, Weitzer and Kubrin (2009) assert that such music is a method of controlling *all* women because it is consumed by a diverse range of young people. In one experiment, youth who were exposed to rap music later reported a higher probability that they would commit violent acts than those who were not exposed. Other forms of popular music also promote violence as the appropriate method of maintaining patriarchal control. While these messages are aimed mainly at males, women growing up in the same society hear the same messages. Thus, some research has found that among African-American adolescents, those exposed to violent rap videos are more likely to accept teen dating violence committed by a male (Johnson, Jackson, and Gatto, 1995).

Even though the mainstream media, for the most part, presents pornography as "glamorous" and "chic," it is not entirely sexist and racist. Some articles and letters written by anti-pornography scholars and activists are periodically published by the conventional press and some feminists have appeared on CNN. These serve as evidence that the orthodox media does not entirely dismiss struggles against violent pornography and other forms of patriarchal oppression (Caringella-MacDonald and Humphries, 1998). For example, pioneering feminist Gloria Steinem's critique of the NBC television series *The Playboy Club*[1] recently appeared in the widely read Canadian daily newspaper the *Toronto Star*. She stated:

> The question is the attitude of the film or series. Is it aggrandizing the past in a nostalgic way, or is it really showing the problems of the past in order to show that we have come forward and continue to come forward? I somehow think the Playboy shows are maybe not doing that. There are other shows that do. I feel dismay that young men especially are being subjected to that and made to feel that's a mark of masculinity.
>
> (cited in Salem, 2011, p. 1)

Sometimes, too, prominent Hollywood figures will progressively respond to issues addressed in this book. As described in Chapter 3, a female Steubenville, Ohio high school student was sexually assaulted by two football players and her victimization was posted on social media, which in the minds of many feminists is a "second rape" (Madigan and Gamble, 1989). Featured in Box 5.1, in the spring of 2014, well-known actor and film producer Brad Pitt owned a production company that purchased the film rights to a *Rolling Stone*[2] article about this incident,[3] and the movie based on it is likely to garner much praise and support from feminist men's organizations. While there are variations in the feminist men's movement, a general point of agreement is that men must take an active role in stopping woman abuse and eliminating other forms of patriarchal control and domination throughout society (DeKeseredy and Schwartz, 2013). One of the central arguments is that one of the most important steps a man can take if he wants to improve women's quality of life is to join the feminist men's movement, which first involves self-examination and self-discovery (Funk, 2006; Thorne-Finch, 1992). In other words, men must be willing to examine their own attitudes and beliefs about women, sexuality, masculinity, and gender relations. This is what Jackson Katz (2006) refers to as "similar to the sort of introspection required of anti-racist whites" (p. 260).

Following this transition in their lives, members of the feminist men's movement need to confront and openly talk to men who abuse women, even if they are friends, neighbors, and employers. It is also necessary to implement strategies like Pitt's and others discussed subsequently in this chapter. However, mentioned in Box 5.1 is the fact that there are feminists who strongly disapprove of Pitt's initiative. Unfortunately, some women's groups have been "burned" so often that they question whether any men's groups can be counted upon as useful allies. Campus anti-rape groups across North America are often split on whether to accept the help of college men. Part of the problem is that many men who want to be involved in the programming still hold and express attitudes that undercut the entire point of educational campaigns. Another cause for suspicion is that, after all, the entire unlikely point of feminist men's groups is to organize to give up some of men's power (Christian, 1994; Funk, 2006; Schwartz and DeKeseredy, 1997). Yet, there are strong reasons for why women and men should work together to curb woman abuse, violent pornography, and other highly injurious symptoms of patriarchy. Still relevant today, one argument is made by hooks (1992):

> Men who actively struggle against sexism have a place in the feminist movement. They are our comrades. . . . Those women's liberationists who see no value in this participation must rethink and reexamine the process by which revolutionary struggle is advanced. Individual men tend to become involved in the feminist movement because of the pain generated in relationships with women. Until men share responsibility for struggling to end sexism, the feminist movement will reflect the very sexist contradictions we wish to eradicate. . . . In particular, men have a tremendous contribution to make . . . in the area of exposing, confronting, opposing, and transforming the sexism of their male peers.
>
> (pp. 570–571)

Working with the mainstream media should also involve academic experts on pornography avoiding limiting their presentations of data or policy proposals to scholarly forums or community groups. They also need to disseminate their arguments through the mainstream mass media, an approach often referred to as *newsmaking criminology* (Barak, 2007). Since its inception (see Barak, 1988), newsmaking criminology has not yet "been taken up to any great degree in Canada (or elsewhere)" (Doyle and Moore, 2011, p. 20). The voices of people in favor of pornography, such as "porn star" Jenna Jameson (2004), are heard the most and thus it is time to challenge this hegemony with some newspaper articles and television and radio interviews.

Barak (1988), among other criminologists (e.g., Corsianos, 2012; DeKeseredy, 2011b; Schwartz and DeKeseredy, 1997), call for scholars and activists to develop relationships with progressive reporters who are more likely to report alternative interpretations of gender issues and other social problems. Making links with reporters involves letting them know that academic researchers are available for comment on breaking national or local news, or being willing to work on the types of newspaper

Box 5.1 A MOVIE ABOUT STEUBENVILLE

Plan B, Brad Pitt's production company that recently financed *12 Years a Slave*, grabbed headlines this week with the news that it had purchased the film rights to the *Rolling Stone* article "Anonymous vs. Steubenville." Written by David Kushner, the piece chronicles the efforts of online activists, flying under the name Anonymous, to get justice for a high school rape victim in Steubenville, Ohio. The protagonists of the article are a bunch of young white men who were touched by this girl's suffering and angered by what they deemed a town cover-up of the crime, and set out to make things right.

You can see the appeal of this story from a Hollywood perspective: Young men go up against a football town to rescue a female rape victim. But Tara Culp-Ressler at *ThinkProgress* is not happy about the male-centric nature of the story and thinks it is typical of Hollywood's inability to do social justice stories any justice:

> In a culture where rape survivors' voices are often ignored, and women's stories about their own lived experiences of sexual violence and oppression are constantly brought into question, it's discouraging to envision a movie about one of the most famous rape cases in the country that places a 'white Knight' at the center. Although it's likely not the intention of Plan B Entertainment, that framing choice ends up further obscuring the real women who are victimized by sexual assault.

But I'd like to withhold judgment until it comes out for this major reason: Rape is one of those issues where we desperately *need* white knights (emphasis in original). Rape is traditionally considered a "women's issue," but really it's more of a men's issue. Men commit nearly all the rapes, even rapes of other men and boys. The phrase "rape culture" that feminists kick around describes, above all else, the way that sexual predators move about freely because men don't stand up to them (or in some case, actively support them). Women can oppose rape until we're blue in the face, but as long as rapists can look at other men and see indifference or active support, they're going to remain emboldened.

[W]hen it comes to sexual assault, we need more men to say, at the very least, "Dude, that is messed up." If this movie ends up showing young men a new model for masculinity, one where you stand up for a woman's right to safety instead of wallow in a "bros before hos" mentality, then I will consider it a win.

Source: Marcotte (2014, pp. 1–2).

op-ed piece and other stories that have been traditionally unproductive in terms of academic career credentials. Interestingly, however, many universities today have begun to see the op-ed piece as a way to get the names of the faculty (and, of course, the university) widely known. Many university news bureaus are not only willing to help with newspaper op-ed pieces on virtually any topic of public policy, but they also are very competent in helping to place such pieces in newspapers around the country. In an electronic age, it is faster and easier to place such pieces than ever before.

USING SOCIAL MEDIA

Whether you like it or not and whether or not you are computer savvy, communicating via social media today is vital for two main reasons. First, many people living in societies characterized by "turbo-charged capitalism" and "competitive individualism" (Luttwak, 1995; Young, 1999), especially youth, spend more time on their computers than they do in face-to-face relationships. As Jessie Klein (2012) observes, "In a culture that values independence and self-reliance to such extremes over connection, community, and interdependence, technology is more likely to be used as a means of escape from others" (p. 122). Indeed, there is ample evidence to support her claim that most socializing among youth is done through electronic channels, but it is more than socializing. Many people today get all of their news from hip-hop, rap, comedy, and a number of social commentary sites, rather than from traditional news channels, newspapers, or magazines. Therefore, using social media will enable more people to become aware of various types of racist, sexist, homophobic, and other types of hurtful practices spawned by structured social inequality and therefore help motivate them to voice their discontent with the prevailing inequitable status quo by electing politicians committed to promoting social justice (Corsianos, 2000; DeKeseredy and Schwartz, 2013). As well, it is easier to influence people to join an anti-porn Facebook group to make a political point than it is to get large groups of people marching in the streets (Rettberg, 2009).

For those seeking to use electronic media in their efforts to stop harmful porn, perhaps the best first step is to visit Stop Porn Culture (SPC) at http://stopporn culture.org/. Stated at this site, SPC's mission is as follows:

> SPC is dedicated to challenging the pornography industry and an increasingly pornographic pop culture. Our work toward ending industries of sexual exploitation is grounded in a feminist analysis of sexist, racist, and economic oppression. We affirm sexuality that is rooted in equality and free of exploitation, coercion, and violence.

SPC's site is rich with valuable information. For example, if you are at least 18 years old and want to be an anti-porn speaker, you can download, at no financial cost, three PowerPoint slide shows for adult audiences only. You can also participate in organized protests, sign-up to be an SPC volunteer, and have access to various resources for students, parents, teachers, partners/spouses, and survivors. Additionally, their website provides information on a series of action alerts. One example related to the annual Sex Week at the University of Chicago. The event was described as follows:

> The University of Chicago is holding their annual Sex Week and is inviting pornographers to promote commercialized sex on campus. Here at Stop Porn Culture, we are fully behind comprehensive sex education, and think that the porn industry is taking away from the creativity of sex. The University of Chicago is selling out their students to the porn industry by inviting pornographers to their campus during this week. It's important to take notice that not one of their speakers is sex critical and looks at porn from a scholarly perspective. There are however, workshops on S and M and on how to be an ally of "sex workers" without discussing the people who buy and sell women. Instead of relying on pornographers and other sources for teaching their students sex ed, the University of Chicago should be focusing on teaching their students to critically analyze the messages that the media, and the sex industry are selling them.
>
> (stoppornculture.org)

Much more can easily be said here about SPC's site, but it can't be emphasized enough that accessing it is essential for anyone committed to stopping hurtful pornography. It should also be noted that Gail Dines, who is liberally cited throughout this book, is a Founding member of SPC and is on its Board.

Other action groups with a long history of utilizing electronic media to implement change have included faith-based non-profit organizations such as Morality in the Media (MIM) (http://moralityinmedia.org/):

> MIM directs the War on Illegal Pornography coalition—an effort with Congress to pressure the U.S. Department of Justice to enforce existing federal obscenity laws. MIM maintains a research website about the harms of pornography and regularly directs national awareness campaigns to help the public understand the consequences of pornography and find resources to aid in their struggles.
>
> (http://pornharmsresearch.com/)

Since its inception in 1962, MIM has also conducted a variety of public education activities designed to help citizens deal constitutionally with the threat of obscenity in their communities and in the media. These activities have included the distribution of print publications, operation of various websites, speaking engagements, the White Ribbon Against Pornography (WRAP) Campaign, and media interviews. Some examples of MIM's work over the years that are posted on their website include the following:

July 2012—MIM reached 100,000 supporters on Facebook. In just 2 years, MIM developed a strong online presence through social media, websites, online advocacy efforts, distribution of graphics, videos and flyers, advertising, and more. MIM grew it's army of supporters fifteen times over in just 18 months due to the increased visibility of this issue online. In addition, through these awareness efforts, MIM has connected hundreds of people with resources to help them overcome the harms of pornography that they are struggling with, as well as helped to educate thousands of parents about the dangers of pornography. MIM will continue to grow its online reach in years to come.

April–May 2012—MIM led a nation-wide boycott of coupon giant, Groupon, as a result of their selling tours of a torture-porn studio. 20,000 people participated, including major companies who pulled their ads. After just 6 weeks, Groupon announced that they no longer do business with pornographers.

February 2011–August 2011—After our Executive Director, Dawn Hawkins, witnessed a man viewing violent, pseudo-child pornography on a flight, MIM launched an effort to make sure that all U.S. commercial airlines have policies in place prohibiting passengers from viewing pornography in-flight. All airlines except for American Airlines agreed to not only improve their policies to prohibit pornography during flights, but also to better train their flight staff on how to deal with such situations.

December 2011–Present—MIM launched the *Safe Schools, Safe Libraries Project*, the goal of which is to get filters and no-porn policies in schools and public libraries. MIM empowers local leaders with the knowledge and help to get their local schools and libraries to improve their policies. In 2012, libraries in CO, WA, OR, TX, and AL installed filters as a result of these efforts. Groups in Arizona led the charge to get state laws adopted that require libraries and schools to filter—this law passed unanimously. Currently, we are working with groups in OK and UT to improve state laws as well. In addition, as of February 2013, there are 170 local leaders working to get filters in their schools and libraries.

September 2011—MIM, with the help of its coalition, successfully got NBC to cancel the TV series "The Playboy Club," which glorified Playboy and the sexual objectification of women. MIM launched efforts for "Close The Club" in June 2011 with the announcement of the show debut that fall. MIM successfully got four of NBCs top five advertisers to refuse to place ads on the show and once the show launched, MIM got 12 of the shows advertisers to pull their ads. Low ratings and the loss of advertising forced NBC to pull the plug and cancel the show after just three episodes.

April–July 2011—MIM got almost half of the U.S. Senate and many members of the House of Representatives to send a letter to U.S. Attorney General demanding enforcement of federal obscenity laws. This led to A.G. Holder being questioned in key committees in both the House and Senate about his refusal to enforce obscenity laws, as well as much more pressure on the U.S. Department of Justice.

2010–Present—MIM launched www.PornHarmsResearch.com, a comprehensive website database containing 1,000+ peer-reviewed research articles, along with relevant news and opinion articles explaining the many consequences of pornography. The website is used by scholars, therapists, and counselors, law enforcement, faith leaders, and many hundreds of concerned citizens. Much research exists today that shows the damage pornography has on marriage, relationships, children, the brain, sexual violence, etc. We encourage you to use this valuable tool to educate yourself and others about the harms of pornography.

2010–Present—MIM launched the War on Illegal Pornography Coalition. A coalition of national, state and local organizations dedicated to bringing awareness to the harms of pornography and getting federal obscenity laws enforced. See www.WarOnIllegalPornography.com

2002–2010—In June 2002, MIM launched a new website, ObscenityCrimes.org, to provide citizens with an online means to report possible violations of federal Internet obscenity laws. Reports were forwarded by MIM to the U.S. Justice Department and to U.S. Attorneys nationwide. As of December 31, 2004, citizens submitted more than 49,000 reports. There was no comparable tool for filing obscenity complaints. The Justice Department publicly acknowledged the value of the site and encouraged people to submit possible violations through MIM, and in November 2004, Congress allocated $150,000 to help fund the project. Unfortunately, in 2008, when U.S. Attorney General Eric Holder took over the U.S. Department of Justice (DOJ) all prosecutions of federal obscenity law violations completely stopped. Mr. Holder refuses to enforce the laws and disbanded the taskforce at the DOJ responsible for doing cases. As a result, MIM shut down the ObscenityCrimes.org website in 2010 and is now working to pressure the DOJ to enforce the laws once again.

For others, innovative suggestions for change must be tied to technology. For example, technology is used to play and listen to music and thus oppositional variants of this art form should be used to challenge pornography and other "crimes of the powerful" (Pearce, 1976), such as state or government crime. According to Kauzlarich and Awsumb (2012):

The Internet . . . has many resources to offer those musically in both the consumption of music and the performance. Free sources of music both for recordings and lessons exist. Instructions on how to build one's own instruments along with videos demonstrating the techniques can be found. Online communities for performers connect musicians with listeners, other musicians, and places in which to perform.

(p. 503)

Historically, music has been an integral component of progressive social movements in a variety of contexts (Bennett and Peterson, 2004; Eyerman and Jamison, 1998; Kauzlarich, in press; Roberts and Moore, 2009). Kauzlarich and Awsumb (2012) remind us in their thorough review of the literature on music and state oppression that artists such as Bob Dylan, John Lennon, and Pete Seeger influenced an unknown number of people to protest the Vietnam War in the 1960s and early 1970s. On top of this, labor organizations, civil rights groups, and other organizations have benefitted from music and there is no reason to believe that activists who oppose hurtful porn can't too.

Many readers could suggest other transformative ways of using new technologies. The chief point to consider here is that communication technology is constantly changing and scholars and activists committed to raising awareness about hurtful pornography must stay on top of it and harness it for their causes. This is not to say, though, that using the Internet should be a substitute for other policies discussed in this chapter and elsewhere. Rather, new technologies should be part of a multipronged effort to alleviate much pain and suffering caused by patriarchal practices of all sorts (Corsianos, 2009; DeKeseredy and Schwartz, 2010).

SCHOOL-BASED INITIATIVES

How can we prevent young men from consuming violent and dehumanizing porn and from engaging in pornographic cyber-bullying? Elementary and high school-based educational and awareness programs about physical types of woman abuse (e.g., beatings and rape), such as videos, workshops, presentations, plays, and classroom discussions are potentially effective strategies. These programs help provide an atmosphere in which students show more respect for each other and change attitudes, increase knowledge, and change behavioral intentions (Bohmer and Parrot, 1993; Crooks et al., 2011; DeKeseredy and Schwartz, 2013). Equally important is the development of school curricula that make gender, healthy relationships, and sexuality core subjects in schools (Messerschmidt, 2012). Yet, the harm done by pornography is rarely included in such woman abuse programs and leading experts in the field frequently point out that sex education in schools needs to move well beyond "the mechanics of reproduction" (Lyons, 2014, p. 1).

In addition to modifying sex education and healthy relationships classes, schools should help female students develop what Laurie Mandel,[4] founder and director of the Get a Voice Project, refers to as "collective courage." She told Jessie Klein (2012), "On their own they won't stand up and say something." Thus, the program enables them to "use voices of courage and leadership—and to work together, so that if they see something happening and speak up, someone will say something too. When they do it together, it really works well" (p. 211). It certainly does. Consider what happened at Sacred Heart High School in Newmarket, Ontario in the spring of 2014. Someone created a hurtful website, posting Facebook pictures of female students and asking viewers to vote on whether they'd like to have sex with them. The girls did not sit back passively and accept this abuse. On the contrary, they "fought back." Their collective courage involved meeting the school principal, telling their parents, contacting the police, and putting posters about women's rights and equality that they created in the school's hallways. The entire school staff was very supportive, but the police's response was lukewarm. They investigated the incident but said "it doesn't appear that there was any criminal activity—such as threats or harassment" (cited Rushowy, 2014, p. 2).

Issues related to masculinity should also be addressed in programs like, Get a Voice, but they are few in number, especially in the United States. As Laurie Mandel told Jessie Klein (2012), "[W]e can't have this conversation with girls if we don't have this conversation with boys. We've expanded what it means to be female, but we haven't expanded what it means to be male" (p. 212). This is hardly a trivial problem. Kimmel (2008) correctly points out that

> in the end we need to develop a new model of masculinity. Young men must understand on a deep level that being a real man isn't going along with what you know in your heart to be cruel, inhumane, stupid, humiliating, and dangerous. Being a real man means doing the right thing, standing up to immorality and injustice when you see it, and expressing compassion, not contempt, for those who are less fortunate. In other words, it's about being courageous. So much of Guyland encourages cowardice—being a passive bystander, going along with what seems to be the crowd's consensus.
>
> (p. 287)

WORKING WITH MEN AND BOYS

Presumably, "well-meaning men" outnumber rigidly patriarchal men who believe that women are subordinate to men. According to Tony Porter (2006), co-founder of the progressive coalition, A Call to Men,[5] a well-meaning man is

> a man who believes women should be respected. A well-meaning man would not assault a woman. A well-meaning man, on the surface, at least, believes in equality for women. A well-meaning man believes in women's rights. A well-meaning man honors the women in his life. A well-meaning man, for all practical purposes, is a nice guy, a good guy.
>
> (p. 1)

But, if most men fit Porter's description, then why is there so much violence against women in this world? Why is there so much misogyny? Why does patriarchy still exist in societies and within families? Why do we live in an increasingly violent pornified world? There are four main answers to these questions. First, most men are rarely asked to contribute to efforts aimed at challenging patriarchy (DeKeseredy and Schwartz, 2013). Second, many men are reluctant to participate in anti-violence in pornography efforts (Funk, 2006; Wantland, 2008). And, third, by sitting on the sidelines praising themselves for being well-meaning, these men's silence supports destructive patriarchal messages, images, and practices (Bunch, 2006). Additionally, how many of these men actually have meaningful discussions with their sons about pornography? It is fair to assume the answer is "not many." This is a serious problem. All fathers should thus heed Katz's (2006) advice:

> Clearly one of the most important roles a father—or a father figure—can play in his son's life is to teach by example. If men are always respectful toward women and never verbally or physically abuse them, their sons in all likelihood will learn to be similarly respectful. Nevertheless, every man who has a son should be constantly aware that how he treats women is not just between him and the women—there is a little set of eyes that is always watching him and picking up cues about how a man is supposed to act. If a man says demeaning and dismissive things about women, his son hears it. If he laughs at sexist jokes and makes objectifying comments about women's bodies as he watches TV, his son hears it.
>
> (p. 234)

So, as the rock and roll group Crosby, Stills, Nash, and Young (CSNY), urges us, fathers "Teach Your Children Well."[6] However, also, as noted in an African proverb, it "takes a village to raise a child." Hence, it is necessary to develop a new type of *collective efficacy*. This concept was coined by Sampson, Raudenbush, and Earls (1998) and means "mutual trust among neighbors combined with a willingness to act on behalf of the common good, specifically to supervise children and maintain public order" (p. 1). One important way of developing a collective efficacy aimed at reducing porn is male leadership in schools and athletics. As noted earlier, school-based programs aimed at masculinity issues are rare and the vast majority of them are run by women who receive little, if any, funding and who devote their personal time beyond their paid responsibilities (Katz, 2006). Consider Laurie Mandel's work with boys. In the words of Klein (2012), her

> small program is powerful and effective, yet it can only do so much. It's effectively a one-woman program, and she still works as a full-time art teacher. She has six people, who help her do workshops, and they receive small honorariums for their work—but it is largely a labor of love.
>
> (p. 213)

It is time for more male teachers and administrators to "step up to the plate" and demonstrate some progressive leadership by offering programs on gender issues in their schools. They can also do a number of things on a personal level (Katz, 2006), such as talking to male students and male faculty in assemblies, classes, at sporting events, in faculty and staff training, and in private conversations. It would also be useful for school staff to employ the following strategies informed by the work of feminist Ron Thorne-Finch (1992, pp. 236–237) and Robin Warshaw (1988, pp. 161–164):

- Confront students, teachers, and athletic staff who speak about violent and dehumanizing pornography in an approving manner.
- Confront students and staff who perpetuate and legitimate rape myths.
- Take every opportunity to speak out against harmful pornography and other symptoms of gender inequality.
- Create a Facebook page about the harms of pornography and how men and boys can work together to reduce consumption, production, and distribution of hurtful porn.

Aggressive male sports teams (e.g., football and hockey) are fertile breeding grounds for sexism and the abuse of women, especially sexual aggression (Benedict, 1998; Burstyn, 2000; Forbes, Adams-Curtis, Pakalka, and White, 2006). They are regularly exposed to messages from teammates suggesting that a real man is not under the control of a woman; a real man has sex on demand and does not accept attacks on his masculine authority (DeKeseredy and Schwartz, 2013). This pro-abuse subculture exists not only in school-based aggressive sports teams, but also in those outside of academic settings, such as hockey leagues organized by local communities. Needless to say, too, pornography is consumed by many young male athletes. There is hope, however, due to the availability of effective anti-sexist training that focuses on male athletes' role as leaders instead of perpetrators. One that stands out in the minds of numerous people working in the area of woman abuse is the Mentors in Violence Prevention (MVP) Model. It was co-developed and conceived by Jackson Katz in 1993 at Northeastern University's Center for the Study of Sport in Society. Although MVP is primarily used in colleges and high schools, it could be introduced in communities at large. Furthermore, given its emphasis on masculinity, educating men about pornography could be added to the agenda described by Katz (2014) in Box 5.2.

We often hear that education is a life-long process. Therefore, education efforts should not be restricted to children, adolescents, or college students. Adult males in the general population also need to be targeted. Feminist male scholars and educators suggest that one effective way to help achieve this goal is for male advocates, who aim to stop harmful porn, to make contacts with like-minded males in other communities to broaden their social support network. Personal experiences and emotions can be shared, which helps alleviate stress and other problems associated with doing feminist work in a hostile political climate characterized by a rabid anti-feminist backlash (Dragiewicz, 2011).

With the support of their feminist male peers, depending on their time and energy, some men are able to work on the dual level of changing individual people and social institutions. Others can only have more limited goals. Most limited of all are those who only privately support the principles of feminism and limit their efforts to creating and maintaining egalitarian relationships (Christian, 1994; DeKeseredy, Schwartz, and Alvi, 2000). This separation of private and public attempts to eliminate patriarchy is one of the major challenges for contemporary feminist men (Kimmel and Mosmiller, 1992).

Box 5.2 A BRIEF HISTORY/OVERVIEW OF MENTORS IN VIOLENCE PREVENTION (MVP)

Mentors in Violence Prevention (MVP) is a multiracial, mixed-gender sexual assault and relationship abuse prevention program and philosophy that has been widely influential in the development and operation of a range of gender violence prevention initiatives in North America and beyond. MVP introduced the "bystander" approach to the field. It has been implemented in myriad populations in colleges and high schools, as well as all branches of the U.S. military. MVP was also the first large-scale effort to engage college and professional sports culture in the fight to prevent men's violence against women.

From its inception, MVP has sought to expand the number of men willing to take a stand to prevent sexual assault and relationship abuse. MVP has been especially effective at challenging and inspiring male leaders in the dominant and multiracial cultures of athletics, fraternities and the military to partner with women to reduce gender violence.

In highly interactive MVP workshops, everything is fair game for discussion: the difference between prevention and "risk reduction" strategies; the pleasures and perils of hook-up culture; victim-blaming; the role of alcohol in sexual assault; the role of porn culture in shaping social and sexual norms; the symbiotic relationship between sexism and heterosexism; the many intersections of race, sex and gender; harassment and abuse directed toward members of LGBTQ communities, and ways to prevent it; and the role of women as bystanders when women are the perpetrators of harassment or abuse.

For more information: www.mvpstrat.com

Source: Katz (2015, p. 1).

The most common activities of feminist men involve protesting, attending lectures and seminars, lobbying for services, and shaming men who make sexist comments and who engage in patriarchal practices. Another common approach is *shifting community culture*. This approach calls for the creation of "shared history" in community through the use of festivals, sporting events, music, and art (Cleveland and Saville, 2003). Occasionally defined as "placemaking" (Adams and Goldbard, 2001), this strategy involves the use of plays, concerts, and paintings that send out powerful messages to people about pornography, violence against women, and other highly injurious symptoms of patriarchy. Such cultural work, including designing tee shirts to memorialize the victimization and objectification of women is done in schools, places of worship, county fairs, community centers, and other visible places with the assistance of community members (Donnermeyer and DeKeseredy, 2014).

Although the activities may appear mundane and traditional, perhaps even trivial, their revised context represents one set of strategies for breaking down patriarchy and promoting greater awareness of pornography by giving public voice to the issue and confronting such public expressions of patriarchy. Shifting community culture in the context of pornography addresses directly forms of collective efficacy that facilitate the production and distribution of pornography and creates, new prosocial forms of collective efficacy that can reduce porn consumption, rapes, and other serious harms to women (DeKeseredy and Schwartz, 2009).

Boycotting is another tried and true approach used by feminist men. Consider some of the work done by the Minnesota Men's Action Network (MMACN): Alliance to Prevent Sexual and Domestic Violence. They developed the Clean Hotel Initiative and its model policy is summarized in Box 5.3. MMCAN calls for encouraging businesses, government agencies, and other organizations to only hold conferences and meetings in hotels that do not offer in-room adult pay-per-view pornography. On top of this, DeKeseredy and Schwartz (2013), among many other feminist men, call for boycotting pornographic video stores, as well as gift shops, clothing stores, souvenir shops, and online outlets that sell misogynistic products that promote violence against women.[7]

Box 5.3 PROPOSAL: "CLEAN HOTEL" RESOLUTION TO GUIDE STAFF ACTIVITIES

Therefore, be it resolved that [This Agency/Business/Council] adopt a "clean hotels" measure. For official business of [This Agency/Business/Council] Board and Staff, will strongly prioritize the use of lodging and meeting/training space that is free of pornography. Our primary purpose is to provide space that [This Agency/Business/Council] board, staff, and constituents will not be exposed to pornographic images that demean and degrade women, men, and children and, secondly, that [This Agency/Business/Council] will support facilities that care about the wellbeing of its community by not making harmful pornographic images routinely available. When booking an event, [This Agency/Business/Council] will assess the facility for its freedom from pornographic images. When traveling for [This Agency/Business/Council] business, individual staff and board members will be reimbursed only when staying at hotels that do not offer adult pay-per-view pornography in their sleeping rooms. We understand that in all instances (particularly while traveling out of state or attending certain functions which "require" on-site attendance), pornography free rooms may not be readily available. In these circumstances, the unavailability of pornography free rooms within a reasonable distance from the business activities, or an explanation for why on-site attendance was necessary, must be documented before reimbursement can occur.

Proposed and adopted: [This Agency/Business/Council] [Date]

Source: Derry (2014, p. 1).

The suggestions offered in this section of this chapter are not exhaustive, and there are scores of other initiatives, many of which may already be in use around the world. In starting up a feminist men's group, however, avoid reinventing the wheel and search for organizations that are already doing anti-violence work and find out how they are doing it. Also, to avoid duplicating what others are doing, DeKeseredy et al. (2000) and Thorne-Finch (1992) suggest contacting women's and community groups to determine what type of new work is required. This helps avoid "burnout," which typically happens when people take on too much work, and it addresses the serious problem of time demands. And, in our opinion, no new feminist men's educational program is complete without turning to Rus Funk's (2006) *Reaching Men: Strategies for Preventing Sexist Attitudes, Behaviors, and Violence.* This valuable reference book includes:[8]

- effective strategies for educating men;
- case studies that illustrate the points being presented;
- doing your work sections that guide educators in confronting their own unresolved issues around sexism and violence;
- sample presentation outlines and exercises;
- appropriate responses to the myths associated with sexist violence;
- concise overviews of the history of the anti-domestic violence movement; and
- specific actions that men can take to end sexist violence.

The insights of Aboriginal or Native men, men of color, lower-class men, men who are disabled, gay men, and men who represent other minority groups should also be taken into account when developing a progressive men's group and when planning events. The insights of women who belong to these groups should also be seriously considered. Unfortunately, most feminist men's groups mainly consist of men who are White, middle-class, and heterosexual. There may be several other groups that can provide feminist men with insight, and thus, at every group meeting, "we should always be conscious of who is not there and that we are not hearing those perspectives" (Gilfus et al., 1999, p. 1207).

THE HUMAN RIGHTS APPROACH

Scholars, activists, and practitioners working in the international gender and development field do not treat pornography and violence against women as unique social problems, but rather connect them to other forms of violence and structural violations against women.[9] This perspective is exemplified below in an excerpt from a United Nations (1995) report prepared for the Fourth World Conference on Women, held in Beijing, China in September 1995:

Violence against women both violates and impairs or nullifies the enjoyment by women of human rights and fundamental freedoms. Taking into account the Declaration on the Elimination of Violence against Women and the work of the special Rapporteurs, gender-based violence, such as battering and other domestic violence, sexual abuse, sexual slavery and exploitation, and international trafficking in women and children, forced prostitution and sexual harassment, as well as violence against women, resulting from cultural prejudice, racism and racial discrimination, xenophobia, pornography, ethnic cleansing, armed conflict, foreign occupation, religious and anti-religious extremism, and terrorism and incompatible with the dignity and the worth of the human person and must be combated and eliminated.

(p. 85)

Such international documents equate pornography and violence against women with a violation of human rights. The human rights approach grew out of post-World War II attempts to employ international law to curb crimes against humanity, such as genocidal rape. There are various definitions of human rights, but the one offered here is put forth by feminist scholar Kristin Bumiller (2008): "[H]uman rights are universal ethical standards that affirm the equality and dignity of all individuals. These rights can be applied either supranationally or to groups and individuals within states" (p. 132).

Feminist human rights activists emphasize multifaceted, preventive measures that go beyond a focus on porn and physical violence to a broader emphasis on improving the position of women in society (Bond and Phillips, 2001; Corsianos, 2009; DeKeseredy, 2011a). One manual prepared by an international group of experts included a list of measures that might be included in a prevention strategy, such as:

- reforming the law to foster equality;
- reforming the law to prohibit corporal punishment;
- promoting equal opportunities and human rights; and
- combating stereotypes in the media.

(United Nations, 1993, p. 95)

Returning to the issue of engaging men in the struggle to curb violent pornography, Stephen Fisher (2011) worked with the Fiji Women's Crisis Center (FWCC)[10] to develop the *Male Advocates for Women's Human Rights Handbook*. Deemed by many to be a highly effective teaching aid, Chapter 8 (titled Men and Sex) is particularly relevant here. It helps feminist male advocates teach men to critically analyze sex myths and how "objectification, fixation, and conquering" is now "a common way men approach sex" (p. 80). Special attention is also devoted to helping advocates educate men about the problems with "pornotopia, the sexual fantasy land" (p. 81).

In spite of such international emphasis on various types of woman abuse as hate crimes and violations of women's human rights, many people around the world refuse to accept that human rights standards are universal when applied to women because they erroneously claim that their culture and religion legitimate violent behaviors. For example, one such case that garnered tremendous mass media attention throughout North America,[11] fueling heated discussions about the nature of Islam, turned out to be one of the more dramatic examples in recent history of *femicide* and domestic horror.[12] Mohammad Shafia, his wife, Tooba Yahya, and eldest son, Hamed, were convicted in January 2102 after a 3-month trial, and each was sentenced to life in prison with the option of parole only possible after 25 years. They were convicted of killing the couple's three teenage daughters and Shafia's first wife, to whom he was still married. The murders occurred on June 30, 2009 in Kingston, Ontario, Canada.

The case was presented in the media and a good part of the public discussion as an example of "honor killings," which led to intense debates about whether Islam sanctioned such murders. The dead included Rona Amir Mohammad, the wife who as cast aside for the crime of being unable to conceive children, and three daughters: Zainab, 19, Sahar, 17, and Geeti, 13. Much was made of Shafia's anger that his eldest daughter had a Pakistani boyfriend, which he felt made her no better than a "whore" and which allegedly explained why three members of the family decided to murder all four people, including teenage girls acculturated to the norms of Montreal, Quebec, Canada rather than those of remote Afghan villages.

An important point to carefully consider is that women and children in intimate relationships are murdered every day in North America, almost exclusively by non-Muslims. Stripped of obscuring questions about honor, the case involved the murder of a wife who was trapped in a bigamous and abusive relationship. The problem was that this wasn't a case of an uncivilized medieval peasant following his values, but of a controlling bigamist abuser living out his modern misogynist values (DeKeseredy and Schwartz, 2013). Islam definitely does not condone acts such as Shafia's. As Sev'er (2013) reminds us based on her extensive research in Turkey:

> Honor killings are a misnomer, an ugly facade that tries to cover up murders of women in patriarchal parts of the world. By attaching the word "honor" to brutal murders of women, people are erroneously led to believe that these are somewhat legitimized, and culturally or religiously sanctioned practices. They are not! There is no culture or religion that directly connects murder of women with honor, or honor with femicide.
>
> (p. 21)

Regardless of strong opposition to applying human rights standards to women, there is a vibrant international women's rights movement, and many North Americans are also actively involved in it. For example, a few years ago in Canada, a coalition of students, academics, and educators created the Violence in the Media Coalition and sent an open letter to federal politicians urging them to change the Canadian *Criminal Code* so that women are protected under hate crime laws. Western University psychologist Dr. Peter Jaffe, the group's spokesperson, publicly told Canadian political leaders that "Whether you are looking at video games or music videos or if you look at pornography . . . there are more violent images and you begin to think these are acceptable ways to treat women" (cited in Rushowy, 2008, p. A19). Not surprisingly, the Coalition's call was unanswered, but the struggle is destined to continue.

SUMMARY

Hurtful pornography is poisoning our society on many levels, and the effects are numerous, which requires a multidimensional response. One method alone will not succeed and the work involved in confronting pornography is destined to be ongoing and ever changing, as will be the porn industry and its collaborators' resistance to attempts to eliminate degrading, violent, and racist sexual media. For example, Pornhub, a widely visited Internet porn site recently tried to paint itself as environmentally responsible by planting trees during the week following Arbor Day (April 25, 2014). The Pornhub site, www.pornhub.com/event/arborday presents this message:

> Pornhub gives America wood. 13473 trees planted.
>
> Help Pornhub support the environment. This Arbor day Pornhub will do what it does best and give America some serious wood by donating 1 tree for every 100 videos viewed in our Big Dick category. The more videos that are viewed, the more trees we will plant.
>
> How can you help? Click below to see the best Big Dick videos on Pornhub. While you are watching some nice pieces of ash, you'll also be helping to spruce America up! (Bushes are optional).

This brings to mind Sykes and Matza's (1957) concept of techniques of neutralization. These techniques provide people with easy and acceptable rationales for committing crimes or violating social norms. One of them directly pertinent to the discussion of Pornhub is appealing to a higher loyalty.[13] In other words, porn producers and consumers assert that while they may have offended or hurt many people, they are actually adhering to progressive environment protection norms, which are higher principles that justify their actions. Consider this statement made by Scharon Harding (2014) in her report on Pornhub's tree planting: "So if you're still in the Arbor Day spirit—and perhaps in the mood for something else—check out Pornhub this week. You'll feel good in more ways than one" (p. 1). To the best of our knowledge, there was no public response from environmental groups to Pornhub's marketing strategy. Also, this isn't Pornhub's only attempt to link itself to environmentalism. Harding notes that Pornhub is also involved with Green is Universal and posts Go Fossil Free ads before letting viewers watch its collection of sexual videos (Harding, 2014).

As Jensen (2007) puts it, those who want to end the pornification of our society "have a lot of work to do" (p. 184). What we and many others believe are effective means of doing so are suggested in this chapter, but there are, of course, many more initiatives that could be proposed and probably have been by others. The ultimate goal is for progressives from all walks of life to work closely together to promote the creation and maintenance of peaceful and equitable societies.

As we end this book, we are left with many questions. We are also left with many visions and hopes. Additionally, we have come to the point in our sociological story of pornography where we recognize that to reduce this problem, we must have the courage to change structures of inequality and social relationships themselves. We believe that the prevention of hurtful pornography is both a profound act of courage and a dramatic act of revolution.

We leave the final word for you. Now that you have read this book, what do you make of violence against women in pornography? What is missing for you? What did you struggle with? What insights intrigued you? What information enriched your own perspective on the issues covered in this book?

You are a citizen of a world riddled with pornographic media. Pornography is part of *your* history, directly or indirectly. It will also affect *your* future. What part will you choose to play in the struggle to curb violent pornography and other patriarchal practices and discourses?

DISCUSSION QUESTIONS

1. What kinds of social conditions are necessary in order for individuals to achieve "sexual agency"?
2. Is "sexual agency" possible when one appropriates patriarchal and hetero-normative sexual performances? Why or why not?
3. How can technology be used to raise awareness about violence against women in porn?
4. How can the mainstream media be held accountable for its overall positive portrayal of the porn industry and its reluctance to report the abuses being committed?

NOTES

1. This show only ran from September 19 to October 3, 2011.
2. Published every two weeks, *Rolling Stone* is a U.S. magazine that focuses primarily on politics and popular culture.
3. The name of the company is Plan B Entertainment and at the time this book was published it had a release deal with Paramount Pictures, Warner Brothers, and Twentieth Century Fox.
4. Ms. Mandel is an art teacher at Murphy Junior High School in the Three Village School District in Stony Brook, Long Island (Klein, 2012).
5. A Call to Men's head office is in Rockville Centre, New York and its mission is to "create a world where all men and boys are loving and respectful and all women and girls are valued and safe." More information on this organization is available at www.acalltomen.org/.
6. These lyrics are featured in CSNY's song "Teach Your Children," which is from their 1970 record *Deja Vu*.
7. One prime example of a misogynistic product that is mainstreamed is a popular shirt offered in 2013 by the Toronto-based Urban Behavior chain and the trendy American online outlet Cafe Press. Called "Problem Solved," the shirt has two panels: "problem" and "solved." The former shows an angry woman verbally chastising a man for his behavior. In the "solution" panel the man delivers a strong karate kick to the woman, literally knocking her out of the panel (Hargreaves, 2012).

8. These features are listed on the back cover of Funk's book.
9. See, for example, Fisher (2014).
10. The FWCC offers support services for women and children who are current targets or who are survivors of male violence. FWCC explicitly views violence against women as a human rights and development issue. More information on the FWCC is available at www.fijiwomen.com.
11. Even the popular news channel CNN covered this homicide.
12. Following Russell (2001), we define femicide here as "the killing of females by males *because* they are female" (p. 3, emphasis in original). Note, however, that that there are various types of femicide. For example, one of people murdered in the case presented in this chapter is a victim of *intimate femicide*. This type of homicide involves "the killing of females by male partners with whom they have, have had, or want to have a sexual and/or emotional relationship" (Ellis and DeKeseredy, 1997, p. 591).
13. The four others are: denial of responsibility, denial of injury, denial of the victim, and condemnation of the condemners.

Bibliography

Adams, D., & Goldbard, A. (2001). *Creative community: The art of cultural development*. New York: Rockefeller Foundation.

Adult Video News. (2005, August). The Directors. Retrieved December 20, 2005 from www.avn.com/video/articles/22629.html.

Akers, R.L., & Sellers, C.S. (2013). *Criminological theories: Introduction, evaluation, and application* (6th ed.). New York: Oxford University Press.

Alvi, S., DeKeseredy, W.S., & Ellis, D. (2000). *Contemporary social problems in North American society*. Toronto, ON: Addison-Wesley.

Attorney General's Commission on Pornography. (1986). *Final report*. Washington, DC: U.S. Government Printing Office.

Attwood, F. (2005). Fashion and passion: Marketing sex to women. *Sexualities*, 8, 395–409.

Attwood, F. (2010a). Porn studies: From social problem to cultural practice. In F. Attwood (Ed.), *Porn.com: Making sense of online pornography* (pp. 1–13). New York: Peter Lang.

Attwood, F. (Ed.). (2010b). *Porn.com: Making sense of online pornography*. New York: Peter Lang.

Badiou, A. (2009). *Logic of worlds*. London: Continuum.

Badiou, A. (2012). *In praise of love*. London: Verso.

Baldwin, M. (1992). Split at the root: Prostitution and feminist discourses of law reform. *Yale Journal of Law and Feminism*, 5, 47.

Bancroft, L. (2002). *Why does he do that? Inside the minds of angry and controlling men*. New York: Penguin.

Barak, G. (1988). Newsmaking criminology: Reflections on the media, intellectuals, and crime. *Justice Quarterly*, 5, 565–588.

Barak, G. (2007). Doing newsmaking criminology from within the academy. *Theoretical Criminology*, 11, 191–207.

Barnard, L. (2014, March 12). Doll with real curves finds right measure. *Toronto Star*, L1, L7.

Barrett, M. (1985). *Women's oppression today: Problems in Marxist feminist analysis*. London: Verso.

Barss, P. (2010). *The erotic engine: How pornography has powered mass communication, from Gutenberg to Google*. Toronto, ON: Random House.

Bart, P. (1985). Pornography: Institutionalizing woman-hating and eroticizing dominance and submission for fun and profit. *Justice Quarterly*, 2, 283–292.

Begley, S. (1995, March 7). Ray Matters. Newsweek, 48–54.

Belknap, J. (2007). *The invisible woman: Gender, crime and justice* (3rd ed.). Belmont, CA: Thomson Wadsworth.

Benedict, J.R. (1998). *Athletes and acquaintance rape*. Thousand Oaks, CA: Sage.

Bennett, A., & Peterson, R.A. (2004). *Music scenes: Local, translocal and virtual.* Nashville, TN: Vanderbilt University Press.

Bennett, D. (2001). Pornography.dot.com: Eroticizing privacy on the Internet. The Review of Education, *Pedagogy & Cultural Studies,* 23, 381–391.

Bergen, R.K. (1996). *Wife rape: Understanding the response of survivors and service providers.* Thousand Oaks, CA: Sage.

Bergen, R.K., & Bogle, K.A. (2000). Exploring the connection between pornography and sexual violence. *Violence and Victims,* 15, 227–234.

Berger, R.J. Searles, P., & Cottle, C.E. (1991). *Feminism and pornography.* New York: Praeger.

Betowski, B. (2007). 1 in 3 boys heavy porn users: Study shows. Retrieved March 6, 2013 from www.eurekalert.org/pub_releases/2007-02/uoa-oit022307.php.

Black, D. (1990). The elementary forms of conflict management. In Arizona State University (Ed.), *New directions in the study of justice, law, and social control* (pp. 43–69). New York: Plenum Press.

Boeringer, S.B. (1994). Pornography and sexual aggression. Associations of violent and nonviolent depictions with rape and rape proclivity. *Deviant Behavior,* 15, 289–304.

Bogle, K.A. (2008) *Hooking up: Sex, dating, and relationships on campus.* New York: New York University Press.

Bohmer, A., & Parrot, A. (1993). *Sexual assault on the college campus: The problem and the solution.* New York: Lexington.

Boies, S. (2002). University students uses of and reactions to online sexual information and entertainment: Links to online and offline sexual behavior. *The Canadian Journal of Human Sexuality,* 11, 77–89.

Bond, J., & Phillips, R. (2001). Violence against women as a human rights violation: International institutional responses. In C.M. Renzetti, J.L. Edleson, & R.K. Bergen (Eds.), *Sourcebook on violence against women* (pp. 481–500). Thousand Oaks, CA: Sage.

Bonino, S., Ciairano, S., Rabaglietti, E., & Cattelino, E. (2006). Use of pornography and self-reported engagement in sexual violence among adolescents. *European Journal of Developmental Psychology,* 3, 265–288.

Bourgois, P. (1995). *In search of respect: Selling Crack in El Barrio.* New York: Cambridge University Press.

Bowker, L.H. (1983). *Beating wife-beating.* Lexington, MA: Lexington Books.

Boyle, K. (Ed.) (2010). *Everyday pornography.* London: Routledge.

Boyle, T. (2007, June 29). Small towns have higher crime rates. *Toronto Star,* p. A1.

Brannigan, A., & Goldenberg, S. (1987). The study of aggressive pornography: The vicissitudes of relevance. *Critical Studies in Mass Communication,* 4, 289–304.

Breslin, S. (2008, October 13). They shoot porn stars, Don't they? 1–10. Retrieved March 16, 2014 from http://theyshootstars.com/page1.html.

Brewer, K. (2008, January 3). The digital divide. Adult video news. Retrieved January 30, 2008 from www.avn.com.

Bridges, A.J. (2010). Methodological considerations in mapping pornography content. In K. Boyle (Ed.), *Everyday Pornography* (pp. 34–49). Oxford, UK: Routledge.

Bridges, A.J., & Anton, C. (2013). Pornography and violence against women. In J.A. Sigal & F.L. Denmark (Eds.), *Violence against girls and women: International perspectives* (pp. 183–206). Santa Barbara, CA: Preager.

Bridges, A.J., & Jensen, R. (2011). Pornography. In C.M. Renzetti, J.L. Edleson, & R. Kennedy Bergen (Eds.), *Sourcebook on violence against women* (2nd ed.) (pp. 133–148). Thousand Oaks, CA: Sage.

Bridges, A.J., Wosnitzer, R., Scharrer, E., Sun, C., & Liberman, R. (2010). Aggression and sexual behavior in best-selling pornography videos: A content analysis update. *Violence Against Women*, 16, 1065–1085.

Briere, J., & Malamuth, N. (1983). Self-reported likelihood of sexually aggressive behavior: Attitudinal versus sexual explanations. *Journal of Research in Personality*, 17, 315–323.

Broadhurst, R. (2006). Developments in the global law enforcement of cyber crime. *Policing: An International Journal of Police Strategies and Management*, 29(3), 408–433.

Brosi, M., Foubert, J.D., Bannon, R.S., & Yandell, G. (2011). Effects of sorority members' pornography use on bystander intervention in a sexual assault situation and rape myth acceptance. *Oracle*, 6, 26–35.

Brownmiller, S. (1975). *Against our will: Men, women, and rape*. New York: Simon & Schuster.

Bryant, J. (1985). Unpublished manuscript, as quoted in Russell, D.E.H. (1995) Nadine Strossen: The pornography industry's wet dream. *On the Issues*, 4, 32–34.

Bumiller, K. (2008). *In an abusive state: How neoliberalism appropriated the feminist movement against sexual violence*. Durham, NC: Duke University Press.

Bunch, T. (2006). *Ending men's violence against women*. New York: A Call to Men: National Association of Men and Women Committed to Ending Violence Against Women.

Burawoy, M. (2008). Open letter to C. Wright Mills. *Antipode*, 40, 365–375.

Burton, D.L., Leibowitz, G.S., & Howard, A. (2010). Comparison by crime type of juvenile delinquents on pornography exposure: The absence of relationships between exposure to pornography and sexual offense characteristics. *Journal of Forensic Nursing*, 6, 121–129.

Butler, J. (1997). Performative acts and gender constitution: An essay in phenomenology and feminist theory. In K. Conboy, N. Medina, & S. Stanbury (Eds.), *Writing on the body: Female embodiment and feminist theory* (pp. 401–417). New York: Columbia University Press.

Burgess-Proctor, A. (2006). Intersections of race, class, and crime: Future directions for feminist criminology. *Feminist Criminology*, 1, 27–47.

Burstyn, V. (1987). Who the hell is "we"? In L. Bell (Eds.), *Good girls, bad girls: Sex trade workers and feminists face to face* (pp. 163–172). Toronto, ON: The Women's Press.

Burstyn, V. (2000). *The rites of men: Manhood, politics, and the culture of sport*. Toronto, ON: University of Toronto Press.

Calvert, C., & Richards, R.D. (2006). Porn in their words: Female leaders in the adult entertainment industry address free speech, censorship, feminism, culture, and the mainstreaming of adult content. *Vanderbilt Journal of Entertainment and Technology Law*, 9, 255–299.

Campbell, H. (2000). The glass phallus: Pub(lic) masculinity and drinking in rural New Zealand. *Rural Sociology*, 65, 532–536.

Carew, S. (2008, January 30). Porn to spice up cell phone. Retrieved January 5, 2007 from www.reuters.com/article/technologyNews/idUSN3030000720080130.

Caringella-MacDonald, S., & Humphries, D. (1998). Guest editors' introduction. *Violence Against Women*, 4, 3–9.

Carroll, J., Padilla-Walker, L., Nelson, L., Olson, C., McNamara Barry, C., & Madsen, S. (2008). Generation XXX: Pornography acceptance and use among emerging adults. *Journal of Adolescent Research*, 23, 6–30.

Chapman, A. (2009). Illiterate hillbillies or vintage individuals: Perceptions of the Appalachian dialect. Commonplace. Retrieved September 24, 2012 from www.mhlearningsolutions.com/commonplace/index.php?q=node/5514.

Chesney-Lind, M., & Shelden, R.G. (2004). *Girls, Delinquency, and Juvenile Justice* (3rd ed.). US: Thomson/Wadsworth.

Christian, H. (1994). *The making of anti-sexist men*. London: Routledge.

Ciclitira, K. (2002). Researching pornography and sexual bodies. *The Psychologist*, 15, 191–194.

Clarke, R.V., & Felson, M. (1993). Introduction: Criminology, routine activity, and rational choice. In R.V. Clarke & M. Felson (Eds.), *Routine activity and rational choice* (pp. 1–14). New Brunswick, NJ: Transaction.

Claus, M. (2000, December 12). Internet changes porn scene at DePauw U. High Beam Research. Retrieved May 22, 2014 from www.highbeam.com/doc/1P1-37925753.html.

Cleveland, G., & Saville, G. (2003). An introduction to 2nd generation cpted – part 1. Retrieved February 22, 2013 from www.cpted.net.

Cohen, A. (1955). *Delinquent boys: The culture of the gang*. New York: Free Press.

Cohen, L.E., & Felson, M. (1979). Social change and crime rate trends: A routine activities approach. *American Sociological Review*, 44, 588–608.

Collins, P.H. (2000). *Black feminist thought* (2nd ed.). New York: Routledge.

Connell, R.W. (2005). The social organization of masculinity. In C.R. McCann & S-K Kim (Eds.), *Feminist theory reader: Local and global perspectives* (2nd ed.) (pp. 232–243). New York: Routledge.

Conseil superieur de l'audiovisuel. (2004, November). Les effects de la pornographie chez les adolescents, 24. Retrieved March 10, 2007 from: www.csa.fr.

Cooper, A. (2004). Online sexual activity in the millennium. *Contemporary Sexuality*, 38, 1–7.

Corsianos, M. (2000). Freedom versus equality: Where does justice lie? In M. Corsianos & K.A. Train (Eds.), *Interrogating social justice: Politics, culture and identity* (pp. 1–22). Toronto, ON: Canadian Scholars' Press.

Corsianos, M. (2001). Conceptualizing "justice" in detectives' decision making. *International Journal of the Sociology of Law*, 29(2), 113–126.

Corsianos, M. (2003). Discretion in detectives' decision making and 'high profile' cases. *Police Practice and Research: An International Journal*, 4 (3), 301–314.

Corsianos, M. (2007). Mainstream pornography and 'women': Questioning sexual agency. *Critical Sociology*, 33 (5–6), 863–885.

Corsianos, M. (2009). *Policing and gendered justice: Examining the possibilities*. Toronto, ON: University of Toronto Press.

Corsianos, M. (2011). Gendered justice through community policing. *Cotemporary Justice Review*, 14 (1), 7–20.

Corsianos, M. (2012). *The complexities of police corruption: Gender, identity and misconduct*. New York: Rowman & Littlefield.

Corsianos, M. (2015). Institutionalized abuse of police power: How public policing condones and legitimizes police corruption in North America. In G. Barak (Ed.), *Routledge international handbook of crimes of the powerful* (pp. 412–426). Routledge.

Coser, L.A. (1977). *Masters of sociological thought: Ideas in historical and social context* (2nd ed.). New York: Harcourt Brace Jovanovich.

Cowen, G., & Dunn, K.F. (1994). What themes in pornography lead to perceptions of the degradation of women? *Journal of Sex Research*, 31, 11–21.

Cramer, E., & McFarlane, J. (1994). Pornography and the abuse of women. *Public Health Nursing*, 11, 268–272.

Crenshaw, K. (2000). The intersectionality of race and gender discrimination. Retrieved June 10, 2011 from www.isiswomen.org/womenet/lists/apgr-list/archive/msg00013.html.

Crockett, R. (2006, August 16) The competitive edge: 1. *Xbiz* http://xbiz.com/article_piece.php?cat=43&id=16550.

Crooks, C.V., Jaffe, P.G., Wolfe, D.A., Hughes, R., & Chiodo, D. (2011). School-based dating violence prevention: From single events to evaluated, integrated programming. In C.M. Renzetti, J.L. Edleson, & R.K. Bergen (Eds.), *Sourcebook on violence against women* (2nd ed.) (pp. 327–346). Thousand Oaks, CA: Sage.

Currie, D.H., & MacLean, B.D. (1993). Preface. In D.H. Currie & B.D. MacLean (Eds.), *Social inequality, social justice* (pp. 5–6). Vancouver, BC: Collective Press.

Currie, E. (2009) *The roots of danger: Violent crime in global perspective.* Upper Saddle River, NJ: Prentice Hall.

Currie, E. (2012). Violence and social policy. In W.S. DeKeseredy & M. Dragiewicz (Eds.), *Routledge handbook of critical criminology* (pp. 465–475). London: Routledge.

Cyberspace Adult Video Reviews. (2005, September 12). Donkey punch. Cavr.com

Daly, K., & Chesney-Lind, M. (1988). Feminism and criminology. *Justice Quarterly*, 5, 497–538.

De Beauvoir, S. (1974). *The second sex.* Trans. H.M. Parshley. New York: Vintage.

DeKeseredy, W.S. (1988). Woman abuse in dating relationships: The relevance of social support theory. *Journal of Family Violence*, 3, 1–13.

DeKeseredy, W.S. (2009). Male violence against women in North America as hate crime. In B. Perry (Ed.), *Hate crimes*, volume 3 (pp. 151–172). Santa Barbara, CA: Praeger.

DeKeseredy, W.S. (2011a). *Violence against women: Myths, facts, controversies.* Toronto, ON: University of Toronto Press.

DeKeseredy, W.S. (2011b). *Contemporary critical criminology.* London: Routledge.

DeKeseredy, W.S. (2015). Patriarchy.com: Adult Internet pornography and the abuse of women. In C.M. Renzetti & R. Kennedy Bergen (Eds.), *Understanding diversity: Celebrating difference, challenging inequality* (pp. 186–199). Boston, MA: Pearson.

DeKeseredy, W.S. (in press). Pornography and violence against women. In C.A. Cuevas & C.M. Rennison (Eds.), *The Wiley-Blackwell handbook on the psychology of violence.* West Sussex, UK: Wiley-Blackwell.

DeKeseredy, W.S., Donnermeyer, J.F., & Schwartz, M.D. (2009). Toward a gendered second generation CPTED for preventing woman abuse in rural communities. *Security Journal*, 22, 178–189.

DeKeseredy, W.S., & Dragiewicz, M. (Eds.). (2012). *Routledge handbook of critical criminology.* London: Routledge.

DeKeseredy, W.S., & Dragiewicz, M. (Eds.). (2014). *Critical criminology*, volumes 1–4. London: Routledge.

DeKeseredy, W.S., Ellis, D., & Alvi, S. (2005). *Deviance and crime: Theory, research and policy.* Cincinnati, OH: LexisNexis.

DeKeseredy, W.S., & Joseph, C. (2006). Separation/divorce sexual assault in rural Ohio: Preliminary results from an exploratory study. *Violence Against Women*, 12, 301–311.

DeKeseredy, W.S., & MacLeod, L. (1997). *Woman abuse: A sociological story.* Toronto, ON: Harcourt Brace.

DeKeseredy, W.S., Muzzatti, S.L., & Donnermeyer, J.F. (2014). Mad men in bib overalls: Media's horrification and pornification of rural culture. *Critical Criminology*, 22, 179–197.

DeKeseredy, W.S., & Olsson, P. (2011). Adult pornography, male peer support, and violence against women: The contribution of the "dark side" of the internet. In M. Vargas Martin, M. Garcia-Ruiz, & A. Edwards (Eds.), *Technology for facilitating humanity and combating social deviations: Interdisciplinary perspectives* (pp. 34–50). Hershey, PA: IGI Global.

DeKeseredy, W.S., & Schwartz, M.D. (1993). Male peer support and woman abuse: An expansion of DeKeseredy's model. *Sociological Spectrum*, 13, 394–414.

DeKeseredy, W.S., & Schwartz, M.D. (1996). *Contemporary criminology.* Belmont, CA: Wadsworth.

DeKeseredy, W.S., & Schwartz, M.D. (1998a). *Woman abuse on campus: Results from the Canadian national survey.* Thousand Oaks, CA: Sage.

DeKeseredy, W.S., & Schwartz, M.D. (1998b). Male peer support and woman abuse in postsecondary school courtship: Suggestions for new directions in sociological research. In R.K. Bergen (Ed.), *Issues in intimate violence* (pp. 83–96). Thousand Oaks, CA: Sage.

DeKeseredy, W.S., & Schwartz, M.D. (2009). *Dangerous exits: Escaping abusive relationships in rural America*. New Brunswick, NJ: Rutgers University Press.

DeKeseredy, W.S., & Schwartz, M.D. (2010). Friedman economic policies, social exclusion, and crime: Toward a gendered left realist subcultural theory. *Crime, Law and Social Change*, 54, 159–170.

DeKeseredy, W.S., & Schwartz, M.D. (2011). Theoretical and definitional issues in violence against women. In C.M. Renzetti, J.L. Edleson, & R.K. Bergen (Eds.), *Sourcebook on violence against women* (2nd. ed.) (pp. 3–20). Thousand Oaks, CA: Sage.

DeKeseredy, W.S., & Schwartz, M.D. (2013). *Male peer support and violence against women: The history and verification of a theory*. Boston, MA: Northeastern University Press.

DeKeseredy, W.S., Schwartz, M.D., & Alvi, S. (2000). The role of profeminist men in dealing with woman abuse on the Canadian college campus. *Violence Against Women*, 9, 918–935.

DeKeseredy, W.S., Schwartz, M.D., Fagen, D., & Hall, M. (2006). Separation/divorce sexual assault: The contribution of male support. *Feminist Criminology*, 1, 228–250.

Demare, D., Lips, H.M., & Briere, J. (1988). Violent pornography and self-reported likelihood of sexual aggression. *Journal of Research in Personality*, 22, 140–153.

Demare, D., Lips, H.M., & Briere, J. (1993). Sexually violent pornography, anti-women attitudes, and sexual aggression. *Journal of Research in Personality*, 27, 285–300.

Dempsey, A. (2014, January 24). Rape threats part of online harassment case against Stoney Creek man. *Toronto Star*. Retrieved January 25, 2014 from www.thestar.com/news/crime/2014/01/24/rape_threats_part_of_online_harassment_case_against_stoney_creek_man.html.

Denzin, N. (1978). *The research act*. New York: McGraw-Hill.

Denzin, N., & Lincoln, Y.S. (2005). Introduction. In N. Denzin & Y.S. Lincoln (Eds.), *The Sage handbook of qualitative research* (3rd ed.) (pp. 1–32). Thousand Oaks, CA: Sage.

Department of Justice. (June 7, 2007). Foreign operator of obscene web sites pleads guilty to obscenity charges. Retrieved February 15, 2014 from www.justice.gov/archive/opa/pr/2007/June/07_crm_410.html.

Derry, C. (2014). "Clean hotels" initiative. Retrieved May 27, 2014 from http://menaspeacemakers.org/programs/mnman/community/.

Dines, G. (2006). The white man's burden: Gonzo pornography and the construction of black masculinity. *Yale Journal of Law and Feminism*, 18, 283–297.

Dines, G. (2010). *Pornland: How porn has hijacked our sexuality*. Boston, MA: Beacon Press.

Dines, G., & Jensen, R. (2008). Internet, pornography. In C.M. Renzetti & J.L. Edleson (Eds.), *Encyclopedia of interpersonal violence* (pp. 365–366). Thousand Oaks, CA: Sage.

Dobash, R.E., & Dobash, R. (1979). *Violence against wives: A case against the patriarchy*. New York: Free Press.

Donnermeyer, J.F., & DeKeseredy, W.S. (2014). *Rural criminology*. London: Routledge.

Doring, N. (2009). The internet's impact on sexuality: A critical review of 15 years of research. *Computers in Human Behavior*, 25, 1089–1101.

Doyle, A., & Moore, D. (2011). Introduction: Questions for a new generation of criminologists. In A. Doyle & D. Moore (Eds.), *Critical criminology in Canada: New voices, new directions* (pp. 1–24). Vancouver, BC: University of British Columbia Press.

Dragiewicz, M. (2009). Why sex and gender matter in domestic violence research and advocacy. In E. Stark & E.S. Buzawa (Eds.), *Violence against women in families and relationships, volume 3: Criminal justice and the law* (pp. 201–216). Santa Barbara, CA: Praeger.

Dragiewicz, M. (2011). *Equality with a vengeance: Men's rights groups, battered women, and antifeminist backlash*. Boston, MA: Northeastern University Press.

Dries, K. (2014, April 8). Horrible new Veet ads: If a lady has hair on her legs, she's a man. Jezebel. Retrieved April 11, 2014 from http://jezebel.com/horrible-new-veet-ads-if-a-lady-has-hair-on-her-legs-1560720940.

Durkheim, E. (1951). *Suicide: A study in sociology*. New York: Free Press.

Dworkin, A. (1981). *Pornography: Men possessing women*. New York: Perigee.

Dworkin, A. (1994). Against the male flood: Censorship, pornography, and equality. In C. Itzin (Ed.), *Pornography: Women, violence, and civil liberties* (pp. 515–535). Oxford: Oxford University Press.

Dylan, R. (2013). Fucking feminism. In T. Taormino, C. P. Shimizu, C. Penley, M. Miller-Young (Eds.), *The feminist porn book: The politics of producing pleasure* (pp. 121–129). New York: The Feminist Press at the City University of New York.

Edelman, B. (2009). Red light states: Who buys online adult entertainment? *Journal of Economic Perspectives*, 23(1), 209–220.

Ehrenreich, B. (2001). *Nickel and dimed: On (not) getting by in America*. New York: Metropolitan Books.

Einsiedel, E.F. (1995). Social science and public policy: Constraints on the linkage. In C.F. Swift (Ed.), *Sexual assault and abuse* (pp. 93–110). New York: Haworth.

Eisenstein, Z. (1980). *Capitalist patriarchy and the case for socialist feminism*. New York: Monthly Review Press.

Elder, G.H. (1994). Time, human agency, and social change: Perspectives on the life course. *Social Psychology Quarterly*, 57, 4–15.

Eller, R.D. (2008). *Uneven ground: Appalachia since 1945*. Lexington, KY: University of Kentucky Press.

Ellis, D. (1987). *The wrong stuff: An introduction to the sociological study of deviance*. Toronto, ON: Collier Macmillan.

Ellis, D., & DeKeseredy, W.S. (1997). Rethinking estrangement, interventions and intimate femicide. *Violence Against Women*, 3, 590–609.

Ericson, R. (1989). Patrolling the facts: Secrecy and publicity in police work. *British Journal of Sociology*, 40, 205–226.

Eyerman, R., & Jamison, A. (1998). *Music and social movements: Mobilizing traditions in the twentieth century*. Cambridge: Cambridge University Press.

Faith, K. (1987). Media, myths and masculinization: Images of women in prison. In E. Adelberg & C. Currie (Eds.), *Too few to count: Canadian women in conflict with the law*. Vancouver, BC: Press Gang.

Federal Bureau of Investigation. (2010). Innocent images initiative. Retrieved April 12, 2011 from www.fbi.gov/innocent.htm.

Ferguson, I. (1996). *A preliminary investigation into offensive and illegal content on the Internet: Deviant criminal pornography*. Ottawa, ON: Department of Justice Canada.

Fielding, N., & Fielding, J. (1986). *Linking data*. Beverly Hills, CA: Sage.

Ferrell, J., Hayward, K., & Young, J. (2008). *Cultural criminology: An invitation*. London: Sage.

Fisher, B.S., Daigle, L.E., & Cullen, F.T. (2010). *Unsafe in the ivory tower: The sexual victimization of college women*. Los Angeles, CA: Sage.

Fisher, S. (2011). *Male advocates for women's human rights handbook*. Suva, Fiji: Fiji Women's Crisis Center.

Fisher, S. (2014). *Involving men to end violence against women: A critical approach*. Doctoral dissertation. Melbourne, AU: Deakin University.

Fisher, W.A., & Barak, A. (2001). Internet pornography: A social psychological perspective on Internet sexuality. *Journal of Sex Research*, 38, 312–323.

Fishman, M. (1981). Police news: Constructing an image of crime. *Urban Life*, 9(4), 371–394.

Flavin, J. (2001). Feminism for the mainstream criminologist: An invitation. *Journal of Criminal Justice*, 29, 271–285.

Flavin, J., & Artz, L. (2013). Understanding women, gender, and crime: Some historical and international developments. In C.M. Renzetti, S.L. Miller, & A.R. Gover (Eds.), *Routledge international handbook of crime and gender studies* (pp. 9–35). London: Routledge.

Flood, M. (2010). Young men using pornography. In K. Boyle (Ed.), *Everyday pornography* (pp. 65–78). London: Routledge.

Forbes, G.B., Adams-Curtis, L.E., Pakalka, A., & White, K.B. (2006). Dating aggression, sexual coercion, and aggression-supporting attitudes among college men as a function of participation in aggressive high school sports. *Violence Against Women*, 15, 441–455.

Foster, G.S., & Hummel, R.L. (1997). Wham, bam, thank you, Sam: Critical dimensions of the persistence of hillbilly caricatures. *Sociological Spectrum*, 17, 157–176.

Foubert, J.D., Brosi, M.W., & Bannon, R.S. (2011). Pornography viewing among fraternity men: Effects on bystander intervention, rape myth acceptance and behavioral intent to commit sexual assault. *Sexual Addiction & Compulsivity*, 18, 212–231.

Fox, J. (2006). Sex differences in college students' internet pornography use. Unpublished Master's thesis, Tucson: University of Arizona.

Freitas, D. (2013). *The end of sex: How hookup culture is leaving a generation unhappy, sexually unfulfilled and confused about intimacy*. New York: Basic Books.

Frontline (2013). The mainstream corporations profiting from pornography. Retrieved May 22 from www.pbs.org/wgbh/pages/frontline/shows/porn/business/mainstream.html.

Funk, R.E. (2006). *Reaching men: Strategies for preventing sexist attitudes, behaviors, and violence*. Indianapolis, IN: Jist Life.

Garcia, L.T. (1986). Exposure to pornography and attitudes about women and rape: A correlational study. *Journal of Sex Research*, 22, 378–385.

Garfinkle, H. (1956). Conditions of successful degradation ceremonies. *American Journal of Sociology*, 61, 420–424.

Gelles, R.J., & Straus, M.A. (1988). *Intimate violence: The causes and consequences of abuse in the American family*. New York: Simon & Schuster.

Gilfus, M.E., Fineran, S., Cohan, D.J., Jensen, S.A., Hartwick, L., & Spath, R. (1999). Research on violence against women: Creating survivor-informed collaborations. *Violence Against Women*, 10, 1194–1212.

Gillespie, I. (2008, June 11). *Nowadays, it's brutal, accessible; pornography*. London Free Press, A3.

Goldsmtih, H.H. (1983, April). Genetic influences on personality from infancy. *Child Development*, 54 (2), 331–335.

Gordon, P. (1987). Community policing: Towards the local police state? In P. Scraton (Ed.), *Law, order and the authoritarian state* (pp. 121–144). Philadelphia, PA: Open University Press.

Gramsci, A. (1957). *The modern prince and other writings*. New York: International Publishers.

Griswold, W. (1986). *Renaissance revivals: City comedy and revenge tragedy in the London theatre, 1576–1980*. Chicago, IL: University of Chicago Press.

Gondolf, E.W. (1999). MCMI-III results for batterer program participation in four cities: Less "pathological" than expected. *Journal of Family Violence*, 14, 1–17.

Gronau, A. (1985). Women and images: Feminist analysis of pornography. In C. Vance & V. Burstyn (Eds.), *Women against censorship* (pp. 127–155). Toronto, ON: Douglas and McIntyre.

Grudzen, C.R., Meeker, D., Torres, J.M., Du, Q., Morrison, R.S., Andersen R M., & Gelberg, L. (2011). Comparison of the mental health of female adult film performers and other young women in California. *Psychiatric Services*, 62, 639–645.

Hagan, J. (1994). *Crime and disrepute*. Thousand Oaks, CA: Pine Forge Press.

Haggstrom-Nordin, E., Hanson, U., & Tyden, T. (2015). Associations between pornography consumption and sexual practices among adolescents in Sweden. *International Journal of STD & AIDS*, 16, 102–107.

Hald, G.M. (2006). Gender differences in pornography consumption among Young Heterosexual Danish adults. *Archives of Sexual Behavior*, 35, 577–585.

Hald, G.M., & Malamuth, N. (2008). Self-perceived effects of pornography consumption. *Archives of Sexual Behavior*, 37, 614–625.

Hald, G.M., Malamuth, N., & Yuen, C. (2010). Pornography and attitudes supporting violence against women: Revisiting the relationship in nonexperimental studies. *Aggressive Behavior*, 36, 545–553.

Harding, S. (2014, April 28). Pornography meets environmentalism: Porn site is planting trees when users watch big d*** videos to celebrate Arbor Day 2014. Latin Post. Retrieved April 30, 2014 from www.latinpost.com/articles/11350/20140428/pornography-meets-environmentalism-porn-site-planting-trees-when-users-watch.htm.

Harmon, P.A., & Check, J.V.P. (1989). *The role of pornography in woman abuse*. Toronto, ON: LaMarsh Research Program on Violence and Conflict Resolution, York University.

Hargreaves, R. (2012, June 15). Urban (mis) Behavior's misogynistic summer wear markets on violence against women. Canadian University Press Newswire. Retrieved June 19, 2012 from http://cupwire.hotlink.net/articles/52847.

Herbert, B. (2009). Women at risk. *New York Times*. Retrieved August 8, 2009 from www.nytimes.com/2009/08/08/opinion/08herbert.html?_r=1&.

Hey, V. (1986). *Patriarchy and pub culture*. London: Tavistock.

Hinduja, S. (2004). Perceptions of local and state law enforcement concerning the role of computer crime investigative teams. *Policing: And International Journal of Police Strategies and Management*, 27(3), 341–357.

Hindjua, S., & Patchin, J.W. (2009). *Bullying beyond the schoolyard: Preventing and responding to cyberbullying*. Thousand Oaks, CA: Sage.

Hinduja, S., & Patchin, J.W. (2010). Bullying, cyberbullying and suicide. *Archives of Suicide Research*, 14, 206–221.

Hirschi, T. (1969). *Causes of delinquency*. Berkeley, CA: University of California Press.

Hobbes, T. (1651, 1963). *Leviathan*. New York: Meridian Books.

Holland, S., & Attwood, F. (2009). Keeping fit in six inch heels. The mainstreaming of pole dancing. In F. Attwood (Ed.), *Mainstreaming sex: The sexualization of Western culture* (pp. 165–182). London and New York: I.B. Taurus.

hooks, B. (1992). Men: Comrades in struggle. In M. Kimmel & M.S. Messner (Eds.), *Men's lives* (pp. 561–571). New York: Macmillan.

Howlett, D. (2012). Sex shops infiltrate small towns. *USA Today*. Retrieved September 11, 2012 from www.usatoday.com/news/nation/2003-12-03-adultbooks-usat_x.htm.

Hsu, S.S. (July 17, 2010). U.S. District judge drops porn charges against video producer John A. Stagliano. *Washington Post*. Retrieved December 5, 2013 from www.washingtonpost.com/wp-dyn/content/article/2010/07/16/AR2010071605750.html.

Hunnicutt, G. (2009). Varieties of patriarchy and violence against women: Resurrecting "patriarchy" as a theoretical tool. *Violence Against Women*, 15, 553–573.

Hunter, J.A., Figueredo, A.J., & Malamuth, N.M. (2010). Developmental pathways into social and sexual deviance. *Journal of Family Violence*, 25, 141–148.

Icon Kids & Youth. (2009). *Bravo Dr. Sommer Studie 2009: Liebe! Korper! Sexualitat!*. Munchen, Germany: Icon Kids & Youth.

Internet Filter Learning Center. (2008). www.intenet-filter-review. Retrieved December 9, 2013 from Toptenreviews.com/internet-pornography-statistics.html.

Itzin, C., & Sweet, C. (1992). Women's experience of pornography: UK magazine survey evidence. In C. Itzin (Ed.), *Pornography: Women, violence and civil liberties* (pp. 222–235). New York: Oxford University Press.

Jacobs, K. (2004). Pornography in small places and other spaces. *Journal of Cultural Studies*, 18, 67–83.

Jameson, J. (2004). *How to make love like a porn star: A cautionary tale*. New York: HarperCollins.

Jenkins, P. (2009). Failure to launch: Why do some social issues fail to detonate moral panics? *British Journal of Criminology*, 49, 35–47.

Jensen, R. (1995). Pornographic lives. *Violence Against Women*, 1, 32–54.

Jensen, R. (1996). Knowing pornography. *Violence Against Women*, 2, 82–102.

Jensen, R. (1998). Using pornography. In G. Dines, R. Jensen, & A. Russo (Eds.), *Pornography: The production and consumption of inequality* (pp. 101–146). New York: Routledge.

Jensen, R. (2003). Pornography and the limits of experimental research. In G. Dines & J.M. Humez (Eds.), *Gender, race, and class in media* (pp. 417–423). Thousand Oaks, CA: Sage.

Jensen, R. (2007). *Getting off: Pornography and the end of masculinity*. New York: South End Press.

Jewkes, R., Dunkle, K., Koss, M.P., Levin, J.B., Nduna, M., Jama, N., & Sikweyiya, Y. (2006). Rape perpetration by young rural South African men: Prevalence, patterns, and risk factors. *Social Science and Medicine*, 63, 2949–2961.

Johnson, J.D., Jackson, L.A., & Gatto, L. (1995). Violent attitudes and deferred academic aspirations: Deleterious effects of exposure to rap music. *Basic and Applied Social Psychology*, 16, 27–41.

Jones, N. (2010). *Between good and ghetto: African American girls and inner-city violence*. New Brunswick, NJ: Rutgers University Press.

Jones, S. (2010). Horrorporn/pornhorror: The problematic communities and contexts of online shock imagery. In F. Attwood (Eds.), *Porn.com: Making sense of online pornography* (pp. 123–137). New York: Peter Lang.

Jordan, Z. (2006). A view at cyberporn and its influence on aggression against women. Unpublished manuscript. Ames, Iowa: Iowa State University.

Juffer, J. (1998). *At Home with pornography: Women, sex, and everyday life*. New York: New York University Press.

Kanin, E.J. (1967a). An examination of sexual aggression as a response to sexual frustration. *Journal of Marriage and the Family*, 29, 428–433.

Kanin, E.J. (1967b). Reference groups and sex conduct norm violations. *The Sociological Quarterly*, 8, 1504–1695.

Kanin, E.J. (1985). Date rapists: Differential sexual socialization and relative deprivation. *Archives of Sexual Behavior*, 14, 219–231.

Katos, V., & Bednar, P. (2008). A cyber-crime investigation framework. *Computer Standards and Interfaces*, 30(4), 223–228.

Katz, J. (2006). *The macho paradox: Why some men hurt women and how all men can help*. Naperville, IL: Sourcebooks, Inc.

Katz, J. (2014). Mentors in violence prevention (MVP). Retrieved April 29, 2014 from www.jacksonkatz.com/mvp.html.

Kauzlarich, D. (in press). *Theorizing resistance: Music, politics, and the crimes of the powerful*. London: Routledge.

Kauzlarich, D., & Awsumb, C.M. (2012). Confronting state oppression: The role of music. In W.S. DeKeseredy & M. Dragiewicz (Eds.), *Routledge handbook of critical criminology* (pp. 501–512). London: Routledge.

Kay, B. (2011). *The urban-rural factor*. Waterloo, ON: Laurier Institute for the Study of Public Opinion and Policy.

Kelly, L. (1988). *Surviving sexual violence*. Minneapolis, MN: University of Minnesota Press.

Kimmel, M. (2008). *Guyland*. New York: HarperCollins.

Kimmel, M. (2013). *Angry white men: American masculinity at the end of an era*. New York: Nation Books.

Kimmel, M.S., & Mosmiller, T.E. (1992). Introduction. In M.S. Kimmel & T.E. Mosmiller (Eds.), *Against the tide: Pro-feminist men in the United States, 1776–1999* (pp. 1–46). Boston, MA: Beacon Press.

Kjellgren, C., Priebe, G., Svedin, C.G., Mossige, S., & Langstrom, N. (2011). Female youth who sexually coerce: Prevalence, risk, and protective factors in two national high school surveys. *Journal of Sex Medicine, 8,* 3354–3362.

Kendall, L. (2003). Cyberporn. In M.S. Kimmel & A. Aronson (Eds.), *Men and masculinities: A social, cultural, and historical encyclopedia,* volume 1 (p. 193). Santa Barbara, CA: ABC-CLIO.

Kipnis, L. (1996). *Bound and gagged: Pornography and the politics of fantasy in America.* New York: Grove.

Klein, J. (2012). *The bully society: School shootings and the crisis of bullying in America's schools.* New York: New York University Press.

Kome, P.J. (2009). Amazon declines to sell "Rapelay" video game. Retrieved February 16, 2009 from www.telegraph.co.uk/scienceandtechnology/technology/46l11161/rapelay-virtual-rape-game-banned-by-Amazon.html.

Kurtz, H. (1994). *Media circus: The trouble with America's newspapers.* New York: Random.

Lacombe, D. (1988). *Ideology and public policy: The case against pornography.* Toronto, ON: Garamond Press.

Lane, F.S. (2001). *Obscene profits: The entrepreneurs of pornography in the cyber age.* New York: Routledge.

Laub, J.H., & Sampson, R.J. (2003). *Shared beginnings, divergent lives: Delinquent boys to age 70.* Cambridge, MA: Harvard University Press.

Laumann, E.O., Gagnon, J.H., Michael, R.T., & Michaels, S. (1994). *The social organization of sexuality: Sexual practices in the United States.* Chicago, IL: University of Chicago Press.

LeBlanc, M., & Loeber, R. (1998). Developmental criminology updated. In M. Tonry (Ed.), *Crime and justice: A review of research* (pp. 115–198). Chicago, IL: University of Chicago Press.

Lehman, P. (2006a). Introduction: "A dirty little secret": Why teach and study pornography? In P. Lehman (Ed.), *Pornography: Film and culture* (pp. 1–24). New Brunswick, NJ: Rutgers University Press.

Lehman, P. (Ed.). (2006b). *Pornography: Film and culture.* New Brunswick, NJ: Rutgers University Press.

Leung, R. (2012). Pornography is a major industry. In D.E. Nelson (Ed.), *Online pornography* (pp. 21–33). New York: Greenhaven Press.

Levy, A. (2005). *Female chauvinist pigs: Women and the rise of raunch culture.* New York: Free Press.

Lewin, K. (1951) *Field theory in social science: Selected theoretical papers.* New York: Harper & Row.

Lewis, B., Fugl-Meyer, K., Helmius, G., et al. (1996). *Sex in Sweden: A national survey on adult sexual behavior.* Stockholm: The National Institute of Public Health.

Liang, B., & Lu, H. (2012). Fighting the obscene, pornographic, and unhealthy – an analysis of the nature, extent, and regulation of China's online pornography within a global context. *Crime, Law & Social Change, 58,* 111–130.

Liau, A.K., Khoo, A., & Ang, P.H. (2008). Parental awareness and monitoring of adolescent internet use. *Current Psychology, 27,* 217–233.

Linz, D. (1989). Exposure to sexually explicit materials and attitudes toward rape: A comparison of study results. *Journal of Sex Research, 26,* 50–84.

Linz, D., & Malamuth, N. (1993). *Pornography.* Newbury Park, CA: Sage.

Livingstone, S., & Helsper, E. (2010). Balancing opportunities and risks in teenagers' use of the internet: the role of online skills and internet self-efficacy. *New Media and Society, 12,* 309–329.

Longino, H. (1980). What is pornography? In L. Lederer (Ed.), *Take back the night: Women on pornography* (pp. 40–54). New York: William Morrow.

Lovelace, L. (1980). *Ordeal: The truth behind deep throat.* New York: Citadel Press Books.

Lush, L. (Ms. Naughty). (2013). My decadent decade: Ten years of making and debating porn for women. In T. Taormino, C.P. Shimizu, C. Penley, & M. Miller-Young (Eds.), *The feminist porn book: The politics of producing pleasure* (pp. 70–78). New York: The Feminist Press at the City University of New York.

Luttwak, E. (1995, November). Turbo-charged capitalism and its consequences. *London Review of Books*, pp. 6–7.

Lyons, J. (2014, February 28). Schools urged to give lessons on pornography and sexting to prevent "distorted image" of sex. *Mirror.* Retrieved April 28, 2014 from www.mirror.co.uk/news/uk-news/porn-lessons-schools-urged-give-3194200.

Lynch, A. (2012). *Porn Chic: Exploring the contours of raunch eroticism.* London: Berg.

Madigan, L., & Gamble, N. (1989). *The second rape: Society's continued betrayal of the victim.* Toronto, ON: Maxwell Macmillan.

McCleary, R. (2008). Rural hotspots: The case of adult businesses. *Criminal Justice Policy Review*, 19, 153–163.

McClintock, A. (1995). Gonad the barbarian and the Venus Flytrap: Portraying the female and male orgasm. In L. Segal & M. McIntosh (Eds.), *Sex exposed: Sexuality and the pornography debate* (pp. 111–131). New Brunswick, NJ: Rutgers University Press.

McCormick, C. (1995). *Constructing danger: The mis/representation of crime in the news.* Halifax, NS: Fernwood.

McElroy, W. (1995). *XXX: A woman's right to pornography.* New York: St. Martin's Press.

MacKinnon, C. (1983). Feminism, Marxism, method, and the state: Toward feminist jurisprudence. *Signs*, 8, 635–658.

MacKinnon, C. (1989). Sexuality, pornography, and method: Pleasure under patriarchy. *Ethics*, 99, 314–436.

MacKinnon, C. (1993). *Only words.* Harvard: Harvard University Press.

MacKinnon, C. (1997). The roar on the other side of silence. In C. MacKinnon & A. Dworkin (Eds.), *In Harm's way: The pornography civil rights hearing* (pp. 3–24). Harvard: Harvard University Press.

McLaughlin, E. (2007). *The new policing.* Thousand Oaks, CA: Sage.

McNair, B. (2002). *Striptease culture: Sex, media, and the democratisation of desire.* London: Routledge.

Maddison, S. (2004). From porno-topia to total information awareness, or what forces really govern access to porn? *New Formations*, 52, 35–57.

Maidment, M.R. (2006). Transgressing boundaries: Feminist perspectives in criminology. In W.S. DeKeseredy & B. Perry (Eds.), *Advancing critical criminology: Theory and application* (pp. 43–62). Lanham, MD: Lexington Books.

Maier, S.L., & Bergen, R.K. (2012). Critical issues in intimate partner violence. In W.S. DeKeseredy & M. Dragiewicz (Eds.), *Routledge handbook of critical criminology* (pp. 329–341). London: Routledge.

Manne, R. (2011). Bad news: Murdoch's Australian and the shaping of the nation. *Quarterly Essay*, 42, 1–19.

Marcotte, A. (2014, April 4). A movie about Steubenville from a male perspective is a great idea. *Slate.* Retrieved April 7, 2014 from www.slate.com/blogs/xx_factor/2014/04/04/brad_pitt_s_plan_b_buys_the_rights_to_anonymous_vs_steubenville_a_male_centric.html.

Marcum, C., Higgins, G., Ricketts, M., & Freiburger, T. (2011). An assessment of the training and resources dedicated nationally to investigation of the production of child pornography. *Policing*, 5(1), 23–32.

Maltz, W., & Maltz, L. (2008). *The porn trap*. New York: Harper Collins.

Maryland Coalition Against Pornography. www.mcap1.com/aboutus.html

Mattebo, M., Tyden, T., Haggstrom-Nordin, E., Nilsson, K.W., & Larsson, M. (2013). Pornography consumption, sexual experiences, lifestyles, and self-rated health among male adolescents in Sweden. *Journal of Developmental & Behavioral Pediatrics, 34*, 460–468.

Mead, G. H. (1962, orig. 1934). Mind, self and society. In C.W. Morris (Ed.), *Mind, Self and Society from the Standpoint of a Behaviorist*. Chicago, IL: University of Chicago Press.

Meloy, M.L., & Miller, S.L. (2011). *The victimization of women: Law, policies, and politics*. New York, NY: Oxford University Press.

Messerschmidt, J.W. (1993). *Masculinities and crime*. Lanham, MD: Roman & Littlefield.

Messerschmidt, J.W. (2003). Diversity in blue: Lesbian and gay police officers in a Masculine occupation. *Men and Masculinities, 5*(4), 355–385.

Messerschmidt, J.W. (2012). *Gender, heterosexuality, and youth violence: The struggle for recognition*. Lanham, MD: Roman & Littlefield.

Messerschmidt, J.W. (2014). *Crime as structured action: Doing masculinities, race, class, sexuality, and crime* (2nd ed.). Lanham, MD: Roman & Littlefield.

Messerschmidt, J.W., & Tomsen, S. (2012). Masculinities. In W.S. DeKeseredy & M. Dragiewicz (Eds.), *Routledge handbook of critical criminology* (pp. 172–185). London: Routledge.

Miller, J. (2008). *Getting played: African-American girls, urban inequality, and gendered violence*. New York: New York University Press.

Miller-Young, M. (2013). Interventions: The deviant and defiant art of black women porn directors. In T. Taormino, C. Parrenas Schimizu, C. Penley, & M. Miller-Young (Eds.), *The feminist porn book: The politics of producing pleasure* (pp. 130–139). New York: The Feminist Press.

Miller-Young, M. (2014). *A taste for brown sugar: Black women in pornography*. Durham, NC: Duke University Press.

Mills, C.W. (1951). *White collar*. New York: Oxford University Press.

Mills, C.W. (1959). *The sociological imagination*. New York: Oxford University Press.

Mills, K. (1990). *A place in the news: From the women's pages to the front page*. New York: Columbia.

Montgomery, B. (October 3, 2008). Pornographer sentenced to nearly four years in Prison. Tampa Bay Times. Retrieved February 21, 2014 from www.tampabay.com/news/courts/criminal/pornographer-sentenced-to-nearly-4-years-in-prison/838305.

Morality in the Media. Retrieved November 10, 2013 from http://moralityinmedia.org/.

Morris, A. (1987). *Women, crime and criminal custice*. New York: Blackwell.

Mossige, S., Ainsaar, M., & Svedin, C. (Eds.). (2007). *The Baltic Sea regional study on adolescent sexuality* (NOVA Rapport 18/07). Oslo, Norway: Norwegian Social Research.

Mowlabocus, S. (2010). Industry, social practice, and the new online porn industry. In F. Attwood (Eds.), *Porn.com: Making sense of online pornography* (pp. 69–87). New York: Peter Lang.

Naffine, N. (1996). *Feminism and criminology*. Philadelphia, PA: Temple University Press.

Naffine, N. (1987). *Female crime: The construction of women in criminology*. Sydney, Australia: Allen & Unwin.

National Data Program for the Social Sciences. (2011). Chicago, IL: National Opinion Research Center. Retrieved March 10, 2014 from www.norc.uchicago.edu/GSS+Website/About+GSS/National+Data+Program+for+Social+Sciences/.

Neugebauer, R. (1996). Kids, cops and colour: The social organization of police-minority youth relations. In G.M. O'Bireck (Ed.), *Not a kid anymore*. Toronto, ON: Nelson.

Neugebauer, R. (1999). First nations people and law enforcement. In M. Corsianos & K. Train (Eds.), *Interrogating social justice: Politics, culture and identity* (pp. 247–269). Toronto, ON: Canadian Scholars' Press.

New York Times. (2012, December 16) Rape case unfolds on web and splits city. Retrieved January 15, 2013 from www.nytimes.com/2012/12/17/sports/high-school-football-rape-case-unfolds-online-and-divides-steubenville-ohio.html?pagewanted=1&_r=o.

O'Connor, L. (Dec. 2014). "Revenge porn" law sees first conviction in California. *Huffington Post.* Retrieved January 7, 2015 from www.Huffingtonpost.com/2014/12/02/revenge-porn-california-first-conviction_n_6258158.html.

Oliver, W. (2006). The streets: An alternative black male socialization institution. *Journal of Black Studies*, 36, 918–937.

Ostberg, M. (August 27, 2010). Vi behover fler kata kvinnor I offentligheten. Newsmill. Retrieved June 21, 2010 from www.newsmill.se/artikel/2009/08/27/vi-behover-fler-kata-kvinnor-i-off entligheten?page=1.

Paasonen, S. (2010). Good amateurs: Erotica writing and notions of quality. In F. Atwood (Ed.), *Porn.com: Making sense of online pornography* (pp. 138–154). New York: Peter Lang.

Paul, P. (2005). *Pornified.* New York: Holt.

Penelope, J. (1992). Heteropatriarchal semantics and Lesbian identity: The ways a Lesbian can be. In J. Penelope (Ed.), *Call me Lesbian: Lesbian lives, Lesbian theory* (pp. 78–97). Freedom: Crossing Press.

Peter, J., & Valkenburg, P.M. (2006). Adolescents' exposure to sexually explicit material on the internet. *Communication Research*, 33, 178–204.

Phillips, F. (2014, March 21). Kylie porn shouldn't be needed for a woman with her talent. *Mirror.* Retrieved April 30, 2014 from www.mirror.co.uk/news/uk-news/kylie-porn-shouldnt-needed-woman-3269461.

Piquero, A., & Mazerolle, P. (Eds.). (2001). *Life-course criminology: Contemporary and classic readings.* Belmont, CA: Wadsworth.

Polsky, N. (1969). *Hustlers, beats, and others.* New York: Doubleday.

Porter, T. (2006). *Well meaning men: Breaking out of the man box.* Charlotte, NC: A Call to Men: National Association of Men and Women Committed to Ending Violence Against Women.

Potter, H. (2008). *Battle cries: Black women and intimate partner abuse.* New York: New York University Press.

President's Commission on Obscenity and Pornography. (1970). *Report.* New York: Random House.

Raymond, J. G. (1989). Putting the politics back into Lesbianism. *Women's Studies International Forum*, 12, 149–156.

Reiman, J., & Leighton, P. (2010). *The rich get richer and the poor get prison: Ideology, class and criminal justice* (8th ed.). Boston, MA: Pearson/Allyn & Bacon.

Rennison, C.M., DeKeseredy, W.S., & Dragiewicz, M. (2012). Urban, suburban, and rural variations in separation/divorce rape/sexual assault: Results from the national crime victimization survey. *Feminist Criminology*, 7, 282–297.

Rennison, C.M., DeKeseredy, W.S., & Dragiewicz, M. (2013). Intimate relationship status variations in violence against women: Urban, suburban, and rural differences. *Violence Against Women.* DOI: 10.1177/1077801213514487.

Renzetti, C.M. (2012). Feminist perspectives in criminology. In W.S. DeKeseredy & M. Dragiewicz (Eds.), *Routledge handbook of critical criminology* (pp. 129–137). London: Routeldge.

Renzetti, C.M. (2013). *Feminist criminology.* London: Routledge.

Ritzer, G. (2008). *Sociological theory* (7th ed.). Boston, MA: McGraw-Hill.

Roberts, M., & Moore, R. (2009). Peace punks and punks against racism: Resource mobilization and frame construction in the punk movement. *Music and Arts in Action*, 2, 21–36.

Rogala, C., & Tyden, T. (2003). Does pornography influence young women's sexual behavior? *Women's Health Issues*, 13, 39–43.

Romita, P., & Beltramini, L. (2011). Watching pornography: Gender differences, violence and victimization. An exploratory study in Italy. *Violence Against Women*, 17, 1312–1330. Retrieved October 13 from http://vaw.sagepub.com/content/early/2011/10/11/1077801211424555.

Roncek, D., & Maier, P. (1991). Bars, blocks and crime revisited: Linking the theory of routine activities to the empiricism of "hot spots." *Criminology*, 29, 725–754.

Royalle, C. (2000). Porn in the USA. In D. Cornell (Ed.), *Feminism and pornography* (pp. 540–550). Oxford: Oxford University Press.

Rushowy, K. (2008, March 5). Hate laws: Protection for women demanded. *Toronto Star*, A19.

Rushowy, K. (2014, April 4). Sacred heart students fight back after offensive website targets girls. *Toronto Star*. Retrieved April 4, 2014 from www.thestar.com/yourtoronto/education/2014/04/04/sacred_heart_students_fight_back_after_offensive_website_targets_girls.html.

Russell, D.E.H. (1982). *Rape in marriage*. New York: Macmillan.

Russell, D.E.H. (1990). *Rape in marriage* (2nd ed.). Bloomington, IN: Indiana University Press.

Russell, D.E.H. (1995). Pornography and rape: A causal model. In C.F. Swift (Ed.), *Sexual assault and abuse* (pp. 45–91). New York: Haworth.

Russell, D.E.H. (1998). *Dangerous relationships: Pornography, misogyny, and rape*. Thousand Oaks, CA: Sage.

Russell, D.E.H. (2001). Introduction: The politics of femicide. In D.E.H. Russell & R.A. Harmes (Eds.), *Femicide in global perspective* (pp. 3–11). New York: Teachers College Press.

Sacco, V.F. (1995). Media constructions of crime. *The annals of the American Academy of Political and Social Science*, 539, 141–54.

Salaman, N. (1993). Women's art practice/Man's sex . . . and now for something completely different. In V. Harwood et al. (Eds.), *Pleasure principles – Politics, sexuality and ethic* (pp. 160–171). London: Lawrence & Wishart.

Salem, R. (2011, August 1). The sway of the '60s playboy. *Toronto Star*, E1.

Salter, M., & Crofts, T. (2014). Responding to revenge porn: Challenging online legal impunity. In L. Comella & S. Tarrant (Eds.), *New views on pornography: Sexuality politics and the law*. Santa Barbara, CA: Praeger.

Sampson, R.J., & Laub, J.H. (1993). *Crime in the making: Pathways and turning points through life*. Cambridge, MA: Harvard University Press.

Sampson, R.J., Raudenbush, S.W., & Earls, F. (1998). *Neighborhood collective efficacy: Does it help reduce violence?* Washington, DC: U.S. Department of Justice.

Sanday, P.R. (1990). *Fraternity gang rape*. New York: New York University Press.

Sanday, P.R. (1996). *A woman scorned: Acquaintance rape on trial*. New York: Doubleday.

Sarracino, C., & Scott, K.M. (2008). *The Porning of America*. Boston, MA: Beacon Press.

Schmidt, P. (Jan. 29, 2015). *A new faculty challenge: Fending off abuse on Yik Yak*. The Chronicle of Higher Education.

Schneider, J.P. (2000). Effects of cybersex addiction on the family: Results of a survey. *Sexual Addiction and Compulsivity*, 7, 31–58.

Schwartz, M.D. (1987). Censorship of sexual violence: Is the problem sex or violence? *Humanity & Society*, 11, 212–243.

Schwartz, M.D. (2000). Methodological issues in the use of survey data for measuring and characterizing violence against women. *Violence Against Women*, 8, 815–838.

Schwartz, M.D., & DeKeseredy, W.S. (1997). *Sexual assault on the college campus: The role of male peer support*. Thousand Oaks, CA: Sage.

Schwartz, M.D., & DeKeseredy, W.S. (1998). Pornography and the abuse of Canadian women in dating relationships. *Humanity & Society*, 22, 137–154.

Schwartz, M.D., DeKeseredy, W.S., Tait, D., & Alvi, S. (2001). Male peer support and routine activities theory: Understanding sexual assault on the college campus. *Justice Quarterly*, 18, 701–727.

Segal, L. (1993). Does pornography cause violence? The search for evidence. In P.C. Gibson & R. Gibson (Eds.), *Dirty looks: Women, pornography, power*. London: British Film Institute.

Senn, C.Y. (1993). The research on women and pornography: The many faces of harm. In D.E.H. Russell (Ed.), *Making violence sexy: Feminist views on pornography* (pp. 179–193). New York: Teachers College Press.

Sev'er, A. (2013). *Patriarchal murders of women*. Lewiston, NY: The Edwin Mellen Press.

Shope, J.H. (2004). When words are not enough: The search for the effect of pornography on abused women. *Violence Against Women*, 10, 56–72.

Silbert, M.H., & Pines, A.M. (1984). Pornography and sexual abuse of women. *Sex Roles*, 10, 857–868.

Simmons, C.A., Lehmann, P., & Collier-Tenison, S. (2008). Linking male use of the sex industry to controlling behaviors in violent relationships: An exploratory analysis. *Violence Against Women*, 14, 406–417.

Simon, S. (2004). Hard-core porn hits the heartland: Rural superstores are "doing great." *Concord Monitor*. Retrieved December 7, 2004 from www.monitor.com/apps/pbcs.dll/article?AID=/2004 1207/REPOSITORY/412070332/1014.

Skinner, K.B. (2011). Is porn really destroying 500,000 marriages annually? *Psychology Today*. Retrieved January 17, 2014 from www.psychologytoday.com/blog/inside-porn-addiction/201112/is-porn-really-destroying-500000-marriages-annually.

Slayden, D. (2010). Debbie does Dallas again and again: Pornography, technology, and market innovation. In F. Attwood (Ed.), *Porn.com: Making sense of online pornography* (pp. 54–68). New York: Peter Lang.

Smart, C. (1982). Regulating families or legitimizing patriarchy?: Family Law in Britain. *International Journal of the Sociology of Law*, 10(2), 129–147.

Sommers, E.K., & Check, J.V.P. (1987). An empirical investigation of the role of pornography in the verbal and physical abuse of women. *Violence and Victims*, 2, 189–209.

Southworth, C., Tucker, S., Fraser, C., & Shulruff, T. (2008). High-tech violence against women. In C.M. Renzetti & J.L. Edleson (Eds.), *Encyclopedia of interpersonal violence* (pp. 329–330). Thousand Oaks, CA: Sage.

Stack, S., Wasserman, I., & Kern, R. (2004). Adult social bonds and use of Internet pornography. *Social Science Quarterly*, 85, 75-88.

Smith, M.D. (1987). The incidence and prevalence of woman abuse in Toronto. *Violence and Victims*, 2, 173–187.

Smith, M.D. (1990). Patriarchal ideology and wife beating: A test of a feminist hypothesis. *Violence and Victims*, 5, 257–273.

Sommers, E.K., & Check, J.V.P. (1987). An empirical investigation of the role of pornography in the verbal and physical abuse of women. *Violence and Victims*, 2, 189–209.

Stop Porn Culture. http://stopppronculure.org/about/about-stop-porn-culture-international/Utah Coalition Against Pornography http://utahcoaltion.org.

Stroller, R.J. and Levine, I.S. (2007). *Coming attractions: The making of an x-rated video* (New Haven, CT: Yale University Press), quoted in Robert Jensen (2007), *Getting off: Pornography and the end of masculinity* (Boston: South End), 69.

Strossen, N. (2000). *Defending pornography: Free speech, sex and the fight for women's rights*. New York: New York University Press.

Sykes, G.M., & Matza, D. (1957). Techniques of neutralization: A theory of delinquency. *American Sociological Review*, 22, 664–670.

Tankard Reist, M. (Ed.) (2009). *Getting real: Challenging the sexualisation of girls*. Melbourne: Spinifex Press.

Taylor, I., Walton, P., & Young, J. (1973). *The new criminology.* London: Routledge & Kegan Paul.

The Atlantic Wire. (2013, January 4). So look who's already in trouble over the Steubenville rape case. Retrieved January 12, 2013 from www.theatlanticwire.com/national/2013/01/look-whos-already-trouble-over-steubenville-rape-case/60621/.

Thorne-Finch, R. (1992). *Ending the silence: The origins and treatment of male violence against men.* Toronto, ON: University of Toronto Press.

Tong, R. (1989). *Feminist thought.* Boulder, CO: Westview.

Ullen, M. (2014). Pornography and its critical reception: Toward a theory of masturbation. *Jump Cut: A Review of Contemporary Media.* Retrieved May 23, 2014 from www.ejumpcut.org/archive/jc51.2009/UllenPorn/.

Unilever. (2014). Dove launches "free being me" badge with girl guides. Retrieved April 30, 2014 from www.unilever.com/brands-in-action/detail/Dove-launches-Free-Being-Me-badge-with-Girl-Guides-March-2014/387373/.

United Nations. (1995). *Focus on women: Violence against women.* Report prepared for the Fourth World Conference on Women, Action for Equality, Development and Peace. Beijing: United Nations.

Ursel, E. (1986). The state and maintenance of patriarchy: A case study of family and welfare legislation. In J. Dickinsin & B. Russell (Eds.), *Family, economy and state* (pp. 150–191). Toronto: Garamond.

U.S. v. Five Star Video, LC; D. Arizona, October 2007.

U.S. v. Five Star Video Outlet, LC; D. Arizona, October 2007.

Vance, C.S. (1993). Negotiating sex and gender in the Attorney General's Commission on Pornography. In L. Segal & M. McIntosh (Eds.), *Sex exposed: Sexuality and the pornography debate* (pp. 29–49). New Brunswick, NJ: Rutgers University Press.

Vargas-Cooper, N. (2011, January 4). Hardcore: The new world of porn is revealing eternal truths about men and women. *The Atlantic.* Retrieved May 22, 2014 from www.theatlantic.com/magazine/archive/2011/01/hard-core/308327/.

Veblen, T. (1899/1934). *The theory of the leisure class.* New York: Modern Library.

Wantland, R.A. (2008). Our brotherhood and your sister: Building anti-rape community in the fraternity. *Journal of Preventions & Interventions in the Community,* 36, 57–74.

Ward, J. (2013). Queer Feminist Pigs: A Spectator's Manifesta. In T. Taormino, C. Parrenas Schimizu, C. Penley, & M. Miller-Young (Eds.), *The feminist porn book: The politics of producing pleasure* (pp. 130–139). New York: The Feminist Press.

Ward, P.R. (2009-07-02). Porn producer, wife get 1-year jail terms. *Pittsburgh Post-Gazette.* Retrieved 2009-07-03

Warr, M. (2002). *Companions in crime: The social aspects of criminal conduct.* Cambridge, UK: Cambridge University Press.

Warshaw, R. (1988). *I never called it rape.* New York: Harper & Row.

Waskul, D.D. (Ed.). (2004). *net.SeXXX: Readings on sex, pornography, and the internet.* New York: Peter Lang.

Web Pro News (2004). Web porn more popular than search engines. http://archive.enterpriseweb procom/enterprisewebpro-6120040604WebPornMorePopularThan SearchEngines.html

Weber, M., Quiring, O., & Daschmann, G. (2012). Peers, parents and pornography: Exploring adolescents' exposure to sexually explicit material and its developmental correlates. *Sexuality and Culture,* 16, 408–427.

Websdale, N. (1998). *Rural woman battering and the justice system: An ethnography.* Thousand Oaks, CA: Sage.

Weitzer, R. (2011). Pornography's effects: The need for solid evidence. *Violence Against Women,* 17, 666–675.

Weitzer, R., & Kubrin, C.E. (2009). Misogyny in rap music: A content analysis of prevalence and meanings. *Men and Masculinities*, 12, 3–29.

Williams, L. (1989). *Hard core: Power, pleasure and the "frenzy of the visible."* Berkeley, CA: University of California Press.

Williams, S. (2014, April 4). Belle Knox's porn crusade is fantasy, not feminist. *Huffington Post*. www.huffingtonpost.com/stefanie-williams/belle-knoxs-porncrusade_b_5042310.html?utm_hp_ref=college&ir=College.

White, J.W., & Humphrey, J.A. (1997). A longitudinal approach to the study of sexual assault: Theoretical and methodological considerations. In M.D. Schwartz (Ed.), *Researching sexual violence against women: Methodological and personal perspectives* (pp. 22–42). Thousand Oaks, CA: Sage.

Whitehead, A. (1976). Sexual antagonisms in Herefordshire. In D. Barker & S. Allen (Eds.), *Dependence and exploitation in work and marriage* (pp. 169–203). London: Lonman.

Winlow, S. (2014). Pornography. In R. Atkinson (Ed.), *Shades of deviance: A primer on crime, deviance and social harm* (pp. 166–168). London: Routledge.

Wilson, W.J. (1996). *When work disappears: The world of the new urban poor*. New York: Knopf.

Wolak, J., Mitchell, K., & Finkelhor, D. (2007). Unwanted and wanted exposure to online pornography in a national sample of youth internet users. *Pediatrics*, 119, 247–257.

Wright, P.J. (2013). U.S. Males and pornography, 1973–2010: Consumption, predictors, correlates. *The Journal of Sex Research*, 50(1), 60–71.

Wright, P.J., Bae, S., & Funk, M. (2013). United States women and pornography through four decades: Exposure, attitudes, behaviors, individual differences. *Arch Sexual Behavior*, 42, 1131–1144.

Young, J. (1999). *The exclusive society*. London: Sage.

Young, J. (2011). *The criminological imagination*. Malden, MA: Polity Press.

Young, K. (1988). Performance, control, and public image of behavior in a deviant subculture: The case of rugby. *Deviant Behavior*, 9, 275–293.

Zerbisias, A. (2008, January 26). Packaging abuse of women as entertainment for adults: Cruel, degrading scenes "normalized" for generation brought up in dot-com world. *Toronto Star*, L3.

Index

as "sluts"/"whores" 80, 87; targeted
groups 25–26; victimization 67; *see also*
feminism
women abuse surveys 60–62
Women's Erotica Network (WEN) 80
Wosnitzer, R. 18
WRAP *see* White Ribbon Against Pornography
Wright, P.J. 6, 7

XBIZ (trade magazine) 3, 14
XTube 22

Yahya, T. 104
Yandell, G. 18
Yik Yak (smartphone application) 74
young adults (aged 18–30) 4–5
YouPorn 22
youth violence 64–65
YouTube 53

Zicari, R. (Rob Black) 32